CASTLES
OF *Sand*

ED YOUNG

● Ed Young grew up in China. As a boy, he was always drawing—even as he dreamed of becoming a pilot or fireman. Today his work has been exhibited in the Metropolitan Museum of Art in New York City and he has won many awards.

● Mr. Young's cover painting has the oriental accent often found in his work. The art shows his talent for using texture, light, and color. The sand looks grainy. The yellow-orange of the setting sun reflects on the water and casts a rich, golden glow around the children.

Acknowledgments appear on page 175, which constitutes an extension of this copyright page.

© 1993 Silver Burdett Ginn Inc.
Cover art © 1993 by Ed Young.

ISBN 0–663–54655–9

New Dimensions
IN THE
WORLD OF READING

CASTLES OF *Sand*

PROGRAM AUTHORS

James F. Baumann
Theodore Clymer
Carl Grant
Elfrieda H. Hiebert

Roselmina Indrisano
Dale D. Johnson
Connie Juel
Jeanne R. Paratore

P. David Pearson
Taffy E. Raphael
Marian Davies Toth
Richard L. Venezky

SILVER BURDETT GINN

NEEDHAM, MA   MORRISTOWN, NJ

ATLANTA, GA   DALLAS, TX   DEERFIELD, IL   MENLO PARK, CA

Unit 1 Theme
Remember When...

Unit 2 Theme

A Watery World

Remember When...

Reading can help us learn about the past.

What events from the past are worth remembering?

SNAP THE WHIP, 1872, *oil on canvas by Winslow Homer, 1836–1910, American. © The Metropolitan Museum of Art, New York. Gift of Christian A. Zabriskie, 1950. (50.41)*

Theme Books for
Remember When . . .

*D*o you like hearing stories about life in
the "olden days"? Even though life in the past
may seem very different from your life today,
some things never change.

✴ When Strega Nona goes to visit
a friend, she tells Big Anthony not
to touch her magic pasta pot. But
there are some things that Big
Anthony just can't resist! Read
Strega Nona by Tomie dePaola
and see what happened in the
little town of Calabria long ago.

✳ The only things Anna brings to America from her home in Russia are her dress and her shawl. When you read *The Keeping Quilt* by Patricia Polacco, you'll see how Anna adjusts to life in a new country and paves the way for her family to feel at home.

More Books to Enjoy

And Then What Happened, Paul Revere?
by Jean Fritz
The Bears on Hemlock Mountain
by Alice Dalgliesh
The Farm Book by E. Boyd Smith
Wagon Wheels by Barbara Brenner

When I Was Nine

written and illustrated by James Stevenson

My own children are grown up now; that's how old I am. But sometimes I look back and I remember . . .

When I was nine, we lived on a street with big trees.

I had a bicycle, and I knew where all the bumps were on the sidewalk.

We had a dog named Jocko.

Our telephone looked like this.
Our number was 3348.

My father had boots and a
bugle from when he was in the
army in the First World War, and a mandolin
from when he was in school. Sometimes
when he came home from work, he would
play taps for us.

At night our mother would read to us.

We lived near a railroad. Before I went to
sleep, I listened to the steam locomotives.
The freight trains and the express trains
blew their whistles as they went racketing
by in the dark.

In our backyard there was a beech tree.
If you climbed high enough, you could see
the Hudson River and smoke from the trains.

No teacher was ever able to teach me
arithmetic.

After school I listened to the radio and
did homework. (There was no television.)

Bill, who lived next door, was my best
friend. He was ten. Bill was pretty good fun,
but only about half the time.

When my brother had a friend over, they
wouldn't let me play. I learned to pitch by
throwing a ball against the garage door.

I skated on a pond in the winter. The ice
would crack with a tremendous booming noise.
But everybody said not to worry.

I put out a weekly newspaper. I collected
news from all the people on our block.

DID ANYTHING
HAPPEN
THIS WEEK?

No.

HOW I PRINTED THE NEIGHBORHOOD NEWS

①   I TOOK A CAN OF HEKTOGRAPH AND OPENED IT. HEKTOGRAPH WAS LIKE A THICK JELLY SOUP.

②   I DUMPED IT INTO A SAUCEPAN AND HEATED IT ON THE STOVE,

③ THEN POURED IT INTO A PAN AND LET IT COOL AND HARDEN.

④ MEANWHILE, I WROTE THE PAPER WITH A SPECIAL PURPLE PENCIL.

⑤ THEN I PUT THAT PAPER FACE-DOWN ON THE HARD JELLY AND RUBBED IT SMOOTH.

⑥ WHEN I PULLED OFF THE PAPER---

7.) ---THE NEIGHBORHOOD NEWS WAS WRITTEN ON THE JELLY BACKWARDS!

8.) THEN I PUT A CLEAN SHEET OF PAPER ON IT AND RUBBED, AND I GOT A COPY OF THE NEWS. I COULD MAKE LOTS OF COPIES.

Not everybody wanted one.

MR. FINERTY, WOULD YOU LIKE TO BUY A COPY OF THE NEIGHBORHOOD NEWS?

NOT RIGHT NOW.

Most summers my brother and I went to visit our grandmother, who had a house near the beach. We went swimming every day.

Grandma was a lot of fun. We would crawl into her room in the morning and hide under her bed.

Then we would pretend to be a funny radio program; she always acted surprised and she always laughed.

But this summer was different. In July we packed up the car for a trip out west. A neighbor said he would take care of Jocko. Bill and Tony waved goodbye.

We drove for days and days. My brother and
I argued a lot. When it got too bad, our father
stopped the car and made us throw a football for
a while. Then we got back in the car again.

At the end of each day we looked for a
place to stay. "What do we think?" my father
would say.

"Plenty good enough," my mother would
say. And we would stop for the night.

My brother and I always wanted to stop and
see something special. Our parents usually
wanted to keep going. "Too touristy," they said.
But in Missouri we visited a big cave.

Our parents woke us up one night to look at
the sky. "What's happening?" I asked. The sky
was shimmering.

"It's the Northern Lights," said my mother.

On my birthday we stopped in a small town and went into a store. My parents bought me exactly what I always wanted . . . a cowboy hat.

At last we came to New Mexico.

We stayed at a ranch and went on long, hot rides into the mountains.

One day we rode to a waterfall. While the horses rested, we slid down the waterfall and plunged into an icy pool. We did it again and again.

It was the most fun I'd ever had.

We drove back home in August. As we turned into our block, Jocko ran to greet us. It was great to get home.

Everything looked just the way it always had . . . except maybe a little smaller.

But I was probably a little bigger. I wasn't nine any more.

Reader's Response ∿ Which of the things the author did on his trip would you enjoy doing? Why?

Library Link ∿ *If you liked this story by James Stevenson, you might enjoy reading another of his books,* Howard.

20

Sky Painting

This is a photograph of the northern lights. You can often see the northern lights in Canada, Alaska, and other northern U. S. states. It's also possible to see them in the southern United States when the sun is very active.

The lights may shimmer or they may stay quiet like a colorful fog. This beautiful sky painting often lasts all night.

Imagine that you are watching the northern lights. How might you feel? Would you feel like painting?

Life in Pilgrim Times

by Carlotta Dunn

About 370 years ago, a group of people left their homes in England to come to a place they had never seen before. For two long months their ship, the *Mayflower,* sailed across the wide and stormy Atlantic Ocean. Finally, in November, 1620, they landed on the rocky shores of North America and settled in a place they called Plymouth, named after the city in England from which they had sailed.

Who were these brave people, and why did they leave their homes in England? This small group of brave families were the Pilgrims. A pilgrim is a person who makes a journey for religious reasons. These people were called Pilgrims because they left their homes to find a place where they would be free to follow their religious beliefs.

In 1620, the Pilgrims arrived on the *Mayflower*.

The Pilgrims Work to Build a New Life

After the Pilgrims arrived in North America, they had only the things they brought with them on the ship. They had clothes, weapons, some tools and books, and a few pieces of furniture. Their food was almost gone, so they had to hunt or fish. Luckily, the forests of North America were full of animals, nuts, and berries, and the ocean was rich in fish.

23

The Pilgrims had to clear the land to build homes.

Still, life was very difficult for the Pilgrims. They had to chop down trees to get wood to build homes. The first houses the Pilgrims built were small and simple. The roofs were made of grasses mixed with mud, and the walls were made of wood. Most houses had only one large room with a large fireplace that provided the only heat for the family in the winter. The family cooked, ate, played, worked, and read together in that room.

After the Pilgrims built homes, they cut down trees to clear the land for farms. Most of the Pilgrims had come from cities in England, so they knew little about farming. If they were to survive, they would need help.

The Pilgrims Get Help from New Friends

Luckily for the Pilgrims, help came to them about four months after they landed in North America. One day, an Indian named Samoset walked into Plymouth, and to the surprise of the Pilgrims, Samoset spoke English. He had learned the language from English sailors who had come to fish in North America. The Pilgrims didn't know it at the time, but Samoset would help them build a new life in their new land.

Indians watch as the Pilgrims land at Plymouth.

The Pilgrim Society, Plymouth, Massachusetts

Samoset brought an Indian named Squanto to Plymouth. Squanto spoke even better English than Samoset. Together, Squanto and Samoset taught the Pilgrims many things that helped them during their first year in North America. The Indians taught the Pilgrims how to farm and gave them corn to plant. Corn was new to the Pilgrims, for the people in England knew nothing about this crop. The Indians showed the Pilgrims where the best places to fish and hunt were. They took the Pilgrims into the forests and showed them which fruits and berries were safe to eat, and which ones would hurt them. The Pilgrims thanked God for their good fortune in finding such wonderful friends.

The Pilgrims share the harvest with their Indian friends.

The Pilgrims learned to read using horn books like this one.

The Pilgrims Believe in God and Education

God was never far from the minds and hearts of the Pilgrims. After all, they had come to North America so they could worship God in their own way. As soon as they were able to, the Pilgrims built a meetinghouse where they came together on Sunday to pray. Everyone in Plymouth attended services at the meetinghouse, and everyone followed the rules set down by the ministers, their religious leaders. It was the Pilgrims' strong beliefs that gave them the strength to build a new life.

The second most important part of Pilgrim life was education. The Pilgrims wanted their children to learn to read so that they would be able to read the Bible. They built the first English schools in North America.

Pilgrim Families Work Together

Religion and education were not the only important parts of Pilgrim life. The family was also very important. Fathers taught their sons how to hunt, farm, fish, build tools and toys, and many other things. Mothers taught their daughters how to cook, sew, farm, and to care for younger children in the family. There was plenty of work for everyone, and the family had to work together to make sure that they had all the things they needed.

Everyone in the family was loved and cared for. Mothers and fathers liked to watch their children play games, and they liked to read to them and tell them stories from the Bible. Life may have been hard for the Pilgrims, but the love they shared and their strong religious beliefs more than made up for the hard times.

Reader's Response ～ What would you have liked about being a Pilgrim? What would you have disliked?

Library Link ～ *If you would like to learn more about the Pilgrims, you might enjoy reading* The Plymouth Thanksgiving *by Leonard Weisgard.*

1620:
A Year with the Wampanoag Indians

Spring is the time to

move to the fishing places.

catch fish as they swim up the rivers to lay their eggs.

move again to the planting fields.

Summer is the time to

plant corn, beans, squash, and pumpkins.

make clay pots and bowls.

put food away for the winter.

Fall is the time to

gather the corn and the pumpkins.

make flour by grinding the corn.

return to the winter village.

Winter is the time to

cut holes in the ice to fish.

sew clothes, weave baskets and mats, and chip stones for arrowheads.

listen to the stories that the elders tell.

Visitors to Plimoth Plantation in Plymouth, Massachusetts, can see Wampanoag family life for themselves.

Over the River and Through the Wood

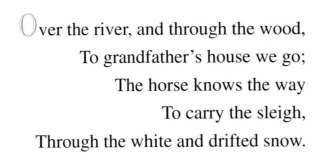

Over the river, and through the wood,
To grandfather's house we go;
The horse knows the way
To carry the sleigh,
Through the white and drifted snow.

Over the river, and through the wood—
Oh, how the wind does blow!
It stings the toes,
And bites the nose,
As over the ground we go.

Over the river and through the wood,
To have a first-rate play.
Hear the bells ring,
"Ting-a-ling-ding!"
Hurrah for Thanksgiving Day!

Over the river and through the wood
    Trot fast my dapple-gray!
      Spring over the ground
      Like a hunting-hound!
    For 'tis Thanksgiving Day.

Over the river and through the wood,
And straight through the barnyard gate.
        We seem to go
        Extremely slow—
        It is so hard to wait!

Over the river and through the wood—
    Now grandmother's cap I spy!
      Hurrah for the fun!
      Is the pudding done?
    Hurrah for the pumpkin-pie!

Lydia Maria Child

31

Grandaddy's Place

written by Helen V. Griffith
illustrated by James Stevenson

CHAPTER ONE

One day Momma said to Janetta, "It's time you knew your grandaddy." Momma and Janetta went to the railroad station and got on a train. Janetta had never ridden on a train before. It was a long ride, but she liked it. She liked hearing about Momma's growing-up days as they rode along. She didn't even mind sitting up all night.

But when they got to Grandaddy's place, Janetta didn't like it at all.

The house was old and small. The yard was mostly bare red dirt. There was a broken-down shed and a broken-down fence.

"I don't want to stay here," said Janetta.

Momma said, "This is where I grew up."

An old man came out onto the porch.

"Say hello to your grandaddy," Momma said.

Janetta was too shy to say hello.

"You hear me, Janetta?" Momma asked.

"Let her be," said Grandaddy.

So Momma just said, "Stay out here and play
while I visit with your grandaddy."

33

They left Janetta standing on the porch. She
didn't know what to do. She had never been in
the country before. She thought she might sit on
the porch, but there was a mean-looking cat on
the only chair. She thought she might sit on the
steps, but there was a wasps' nest up under the
roof. The wasps looked meaner than the cat.
Some chickens were taking a dust-bath
in the yard. When Janetta came near,
they made mean sounds at her.

Janetta walked away. She watched the ground
for bugs and snakes. All at once a giant animal
came out of the broken-down shed. It came
straight toward Janetta, and it was moving fast.
Janetta turned and ran. She ran past the chickens
and the wasps' nest and the mean-looking cat.

She ran into the house.

"There's a giant animal out there," she said.

Grandaddy looked surprised. "First I knew of it," he said.

"It has long legs and long ears and a real long nose," said Janetta.

Momma laughed. "Sounds like the mule," she said.

"Could be," said Grandaddy. "That mule's a tall mule."

"It chased me," said Janetta.

"It won't hurt you," Momma said. "Go back outside and make friends." But Janetta wouldn't go back outside.

"Nothing out there likes me," she said.

CHAPTER TWO

After dark Momma and Grandaddy and Janetta sat out on the steps. The mean-looking cat wasn't anywhere around. Janetta hoped the wasps were asleep. She was beginning to feel sleepy herself. Then a terrible sound from the woods brought her wide awake.

"Was that the mule?" she asked.

"That was just an old hoot owl singing his song," said Grandaddy.

"It didn't sound like singing to me," said Janetta.

"If you were an owl, you'd be tapping your feet," said Grandaddy.

They sat and listened to the owl, and then Grandaddy said, "It was just this kind of night when the star fell into the yard."

"What star?" asked Janetta.

"Now, Daddy," said Momma.

"It's a fact," said Grandaddy. "It landed with a thump, and it looked all around, and it said, 'Where am I?'"

"You mean stars speak English?" asked Janetta.

"I guess they do," said Grandaddy, "because English is all I know, and I understood that star just fine."

"What did you say to the star?" asked Janetta.

Grandaddy said, "I told that star, 'You're in the United States of America,' and the star said, 'No, I mean what planet is this?' and I said, 'This is the planet Earth.'"

"Stop talking foolishness to that child," Momma said.

"What did the star say?" asked Janetta.

"The star said it didn't want to be on the planet Earth," said Grandaddy. "It said it wanted to get back up in the sky where it came from."

"So what did you do, Grandaddy?" Janetta asked.

"Nothing," said Grandaddy, "because just then the star saw my old mule."

"Was the star scared?" Janetta asked.

"Not a bit," said Grandaddy. "The star said, 'Can that mule jump?' and I said, 'Fair, for a mule,' and the star said, 'Good enough.' Then the star hopped up on the mule's back and said, 'Jump.'"

Momma said, "Now, you just stop that talk."

"Don't stop, Grandaddy," said Janetta.

"Well," Grandaddy said, "the mule jumped, and when they were high enough up, the star hopped off and the mule came back down again."

"Was the mule all right?" asked Janetta.

"It was thoughtful for a few days, that's all," said Grandaddy.

Janetta stared up at the sky. "Which star was it, Grandaddy?" she asked.

"Now, Janetta," Momma said, "you know that's a made-up story."

Grandaddy looked up at the stars. "I used to know," he said, "but I'm not sure anymore."

"I bet the mule remembers," Janetta said.

"It very likely does," said Grandaddy.

From somewhere in the bushes some cats began to yowl. "That's just the worst sound I know," Momma said. "Janetta, chase those cats."

"They're just singing their songs," said Grandaddy.

"That's right, Momma," said Janetta. "If you were a cat, you'd be tapping your feet."

Momma laughed and shook her head. "One of you is as bad as the other," she said.

CHAPTER THREE

The next day Grandaddy and Janetta went fishing. Janetta had never been fishing before. She didn't like it when Grandaddy put a worm on the hook.

"Doesn't that hurt him?" she asked.

"I'll ask him," said Grandaddy. He held the
worm up in front of his face. "Worm, how do you
feel about this hook?" he asked. He held the
worm up to his ear and listened. Then he said to
Janetta, "It's all right. That worm says there's
nothing he'd rather do than fish."

"I want to hear him say that," Janetta said.
She took the worm and held it up to her ear.
"He's not saying anything," she said.

"That worm is shy," said Grandaddy. "But I
know he just can't wait to go fishing."

Grandaddy threw the line into the water. It wasn't long before he caught a fish. Then he gave Janetta the pole so that she could try. She threw the line in, and before long she had a fish, too. It was just a little fish. Janetta looked at it lying on the bank. It was moving its fins and opening and closing its mouth.

"I think it's trying to talk," Janetta said.

"It may be, at that," said Grandaddy. He held the fish up to his ear. "It says, 'Cook me with plenty of cornmeal,'" said Grandaddy.

"I want to hear it say that," said Janetta.

"Can you understand fish-talk?" asked Grandaddy.

"I don't know," said Janetta.

"Well, all that fish can talk is fish-talk," said Grandaddy.

Janetta held the fish up to her ear and listened. "It says, 'Throw me back,'" Janetta said.

Grandaddy looked surprised. "Is that a fact?" he asked.

"Clear as anything," said Janetta.

"Well, then I guess you'd better throw it back," said Grandaddy.

Janetta dropped the little fish into the water and watched it swim away. Grandaddy threw the line back in and began to fish again. "I never saw anybody learn fish-talk so fast," he said.

"I'm going to learn worm-talk next," said Janetta.

40

When they had enough fish for supper, Janetta and Grandaddy walked on home. The mean-looking cat came running to meet them. He purred loud purrs and rubbed against their legs.

"I didn't know that cat was friendly," Janetta said.

"He's friendly when you've been fishing," said Grandaddy.

The mule came out of the shed and walked toward them with its ears straight up. Janetta didn't know whether to run or not. The mule walked up to her and pushed her with its nose. Janetta was sorry she hadn't run.

"What do you know," Grandaddy said. "That old mule likes you."

"How can you tell?" Janetta asked.

"It only pushes you that way if it likes you," said Grandaddy.

"Really?" asked Janetta.

"It's a fact," said Grandaddy. "Up until now that mule has only pushed me and the cat and one of the chickens." Janetta was glad she hadn't run. She reached out her hand and touched the mule's nose.

"Grandaddy," she said, "What's the mule's name?"

"Never needed one," said Grandaddy. "It's the only mule around."

"Can I name it?" asked Janetta.

"You surely can," said Grandaddy.

Janetta thought. "I could call it Nosey," she said.

"That would suit that mule fine," said Grandaddy.

Janetta thought some more. "Maybe I'll call it Beauty," she said.

"That's a name I never would have thought of," said Grandaddy.

The mule gave Janetta another push. "This mule really likes me," Janetta said. "It must know I'm going to give it a name."

"You don't have to give it anything," said Grandaddy. "That mule just likes you for your own self."

CHAPTER FIVE

After supper Grandaddy and Momma and Janetta sat out on the steps and watched the night come on. The stars began to show themselves, one by one.

"Now I know what I'll name that mule," Janetta said. "I'll call it Star."

"Should have thought of that myself," said Grandaddy.

"Tomorrow I'll give the cat a name," said Janetta.

"Only fair, now the mule has one," said Grandaddy.

"After I get to know the chickens, I'll name them, too," said Janetta. "Then you'll be able to call them when you want them."

"That'll be handy," said Grandaddy.

"You'll be naming the hoot owl next," Momma said.

"I've been thinking about it," said Janetta.

Momma laughed, and Grandaddy did, too.

"Now, how did we get along around here before you came?" he asked.

"I've been wondering that, too, Grandaddy," said Janetta.

Reader's Response ∽ Do you think you would like it at Grandaddy's place? Why or why not?

THE ART OF
James Stevenson

James Stevenson says, "I think that my experience and creative mind have been formed much more by movies and comic books. I like the idea of a storyboard and I like the idea of a movie and all the different angles from which things can be viewed."

As you can see, he drew this picture with a black pencil and then added color. He also often makes his illustrations look like cartoons or comic strips by putting the drawings in boxes and using speech balloons.

Sometimes James Stevenson draws illustrations in a different way. In the books *Higher on the Door* and *When I Was Nine*, he uses spots of color to suggest the characters and everyday things. He doesn't add the details. He makes readers use their imaginations.

Which of these illustrations do you like better?

The White Stallion

written by Elizabeth Shub
illustrated by Rachel Isadora

This is a true story, Gretchen. My grandmother Gretchen, your great-great-grandmother, told it to me. She was as young as you are when it happened. She was as old as I am when I heard it from her.

It was 1845. Three families were on their way West. They planned to settle there. They traveled in covered wagons. Each wagon was drawn by four horses. Conestoga wagons they were called.

Gretchen and her family were in the last wagon. Mother and Father sat on the driver's seat. The children were inside with the household goods.

Bedding, blankets, pots and pans, a table, chairs, a dresser took up most of the space. There was not much room left for Trudy, John, Billy, and Gretchen. Gretchen was the youngest.

Behind the wagon walked Anna, their old mare.
She was not tied to the wagon but followed faithfully.
She carried two sacks of corn meal on her back.

It was hot in the noonday sun. The children were
cranky and bored. The wagon cover shaded them, but
little air came in through the openings at front and back.

John kicked Billy. Billy pushed him, and he
bumped Gretchen. Trudy, the oldest, who was trying to
read, scolded them.

Their quarrel was interrupted by Father's voice.
"Quick, everybody, look out! There's a herd of
mustangs." The children clambered to the back of the
wagon.

In the distance they could see the wild horses. The
horses galloped swiftly and in minutes were out of sight.

"Look at Anna," John said. The old mare stood rigid. She had turned her head toward the mustangs. Her usually floppy ears were lifted high. The wagon had moved some distance before Anna trotted after it.

It was hotter than ever inside.

"Father," Gretchen called, "may I ride on Anna for a while?"

Father stopped the wagon and came to the back. He lifted Gretchen onto the mare. The meal sacks made a comfortable seat. He tied her securely so that she would not fall off.

As they moved on, Gretchen fell asleep, lulled by the warmth of the sun. They were following a trail in Texas along the Guadalupe River. The rear wheel of the first wagon hit a boulder, and the axle broke. The whole train stopped. Anna strayed away, with Gretchen sleeping on her back. No one noticed.

The travelers made camp. Children were sent for firewood and for water from the river. The women prepared food.

It was not until the axle had been fixed and they were ready to eat that Gretchen and Anna were missed.

The men tried to follow the mare's tracks but soon lost them. It was getting dark. There was nothing to do but remain where they were. They would search again at the first sign of light.

Faithful Anna, they thought, would return. She probably had discovered a rich patch of mesquite grass. She would come back when she had eaten all she wanted.

Gretchen awoke to the sound of lapping. Anna was drinking noisily from a stream. A short distance away stood a herd of ten or twelve wild horses. They were brownish in color. Some had darker brown stripes down their backs. Others had dark markings on their legs. They were mares.

After Anna had finished drinking, she moved
toward them. And they walked forward as if to greet
her. When they came close, they neighed and nickered.

They crossed necks with Anna, nuzzled her and
rubbed against her. They were so friendly that Gretchen
was not afraid. And she did not realize that Anna had
wandered far from the wagon train.

Suddenly the horses began to nibble at the sacks on
Anna's back. They had smelled the corn meal. In their
eagerness they nipped Gretchen's legs. Gretchen
screamed. She tried to move
out of the way. She tried
to loosen the ropes that tied
her. But she could not reach
the knots. Terrified, Gretchen
screamed and screamed.

Out of nowhere a great
white stallion appeared. He
pranced and whinnied. He
swished his long white tail.
He stood on his hind legs,
his white mane flying.

The mares moved quickly out of his way.
The white stallion came up to Anna. He carefully
bit through the ropes that tied Gretchen. Then, gently,
he took hold of the back of her dress with his teeth.
He lifted her to the ground.

He seemed to motion to the mares with his head, and then he galloped away. The mares followed at once. Anna followed them. Gretchen was left alone.

She did not know what to do. ''Father will find me soon,'' she said out loud to comfort herself. She was hungry, but there was nothing to eat. She walked to the stream and drank some water. Then she sat down on a rock to wait.

She waited and waited, but there was no sign of Father. And no sign of Anna. Shadows began to fall. The sun went down. The dark came. ''Anna!'' Gretchen called. ''Anna! Anna! Anna!''

There was no answering sound. She heard a coyote howl. She heard the rustling of leaves and the call of redbirds. Gretchen began to cry.

She made a place for herself on some dry leaves near a tree trunk. She curled up against it, and cried and cried until she fell asleep.

Morning light woke Gretchen. The stream sparkled in the sunlight. Gretchen washed her face and drank the clear water.

She looked for Anna. She called her name, but Anna did not come. Gretchen was so hungry she chewed some sweet grass. But it had a nasty taste, and she spat it out.

She sat on her rock near the stream. She looked at the red bite marks on her legs and began to cry again.

A squirrel came by. It looked at her in such a funny way that she stopped crying.

She walked along the stream. She knew she must not go far. "If you are lost," Mother had warned, "stay where you are. That will make it easier to find you." Gretchen walked back to her rock.

It was afternoon when she heard the sound of hooves. A moment later Anna ambled up to the stream. The sacks of meal were gone. The old mare drank greedily. Gretchen hugged and kissed her. She patted her back. Anna would find her way back to the wagon train.

She tried to climb on Anna's back, but even without the sacks the mare was too high. There was a fallen tree not far away. Gretchen wanted to use it as a step. She tugged at Anna, but Anna would not move. Gretchen pulled and shoved. She begged and pleaded. Anna stood firm.

Now again the white stallion appeared. Again he lifted Gretchen by the back of her dress. He sat her on Anna's back. He nuzzled and pushed the old mare. Anna began to walk. The white stallion walked close behind her for a few paces. Then, as if to say goodbye, he stood on his hind legs, whinnied, and galloped away.

Gretchen always believed the white stallion had told Anna to take her back to the wagon train. For that is what Anna did.

Your great-great-grandmother Gretchen bore the scars of the wild mare bites for the rest of her life. I know because when she told me the story, she pulled down her stockings. And I saw them.

Reader's Response ∾ Do you think Gretchen acted wisely when she became separated from her family? What would you have done?

Library Link ∾ *If you enjoyed this story, you might want to read* The Girl Who Loved Wild Horses *by Paul Goble.*

The MUSTANG TRAIL

Five hundred years ago the Indians of the Southwest had never even seen a horse.

Spanish explorers brought horses to the Americas during the 1500s. These horses were tame but grew wild after they escaped or were set free to roam the western plains.

In the 1800s, there were millions of wild mustangs in the United States.

As people moved West making farms and towns, the number of wild horses dropped.

By the 1960s, there were so few wild mustangs left that people feared they'd disappear completely.

School children just like you wrote to Congress asking for help. It worked! In 1971 Congress passed a law to protect these wild horses.

Today, there are 44,000 wild mustangs in the western plains of the United States, mostly in the sagebrush deserts of Nevada and Wyoming.

Children of Long Ago

The children who lived a long time ago
In little country towns
Ate picnics under spreading trees,
Played hopscotch on the cool dirt yards,
Picked juicy grapes from broad grapevines,
Pulled beets and potatoes from the ground,
Those children of long ago.

The children who lived a long time ago
In little country towns
Tromped to school on hard-frozen roads,
Warmed themselves by wood-burning stoves,
Ate supper by light from oil-filled lamps,
Built fancy snowmen dressed like clowns,
Those children of long ago.

The children who lived a long time ago
In little country towns
Decked themselves in their Sunday best,
Went to church and visited friends,
Sang happy songs with their mamas and papas,
Traveled through books for sights and sounds,
Those children of long ago.

Lessie Jones Little
Jan Spivey Gilchrist, *illustrator*

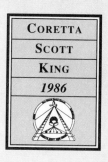

·THE·
PATCHWORK QUILT
by VALERIE FLOURNOY
pictures by JERRY PINKNEY

Tanya sat restlessly on her chair by the kitchen window. For several days she had had to stay in bed with a cold. But now Tanya's cold was almost gone. She was anxious to go outside and enjoy the fresh air and the arrival of spring.

"Mama, when can I go outside?" asked Tanya. Mama pulled the tray of biscuits from the oven and placed it on the counter.

"In time," she murmured. "All in good time."

Tanya gazed through the window and saw her two brothers, Ted and Jim, and Papa building the new backyard fence.

"I'm gonna talk to Grandma," she said.

Grandma was sitting in her favorite spot—the big soft chair in front of the picture window. In her lap were scraps of materials of all textures and colors. Tanya recognized some of them. The plaid was from Papa's old work shirt, and the red scraps were from the shirt Ted had torn that winter.

"Whatcha gonna do with all that stuff?" Tanya asked.

59

"Stuff? These ain't stuff. These little pieces gonna make me a quilt, a patchwork quilt."

Tanya tilted her head. "I know what a quilt is, Grandma. There's one on your bed, but it's old and dirty and Mama can never get it clean."

Grandma sighed. "It ain't dirty, honey. It's worn, the way it's supposed to be."

Grandma flexed her fingers to keep them from stiffening. She sucked in some air and said, "My mother made me a quilt when I wasn't any older than you. But sometimes the old ways are forgotten."

Tanya leaned against the chair and rested her head on her grandmother's shoulder.

Just then Mama walked in with two glasses of milk and some biscuits. Mama looked at the scraps of material that were scattered all over. "Grandma," she said, "I just cleaned this room, and now it's a mess."

"It's not a mess, Mama," Tanya said through a mouthful of biscuit. "It's a quilt."

"A quilt! You don't need these scraps. I can get you a quilt," Mama said.

Grandma looked at her daughter and then turned to her grandchild. "Yes, your mama can get you a quilt from any department store. But it won't be like my patchwork quilt, and it won't last as long either."

Mama looked at Grandma, then picked up Tanya's empty glass and went to make lunch.

Grandma's eyes grew dark and distant. She
turned away from Tanya and gazed out the
window, absentmindedly rubbing the pieces of
material through her fingers.

"Grandma, I'll help you make your quilt,"
Tanya said.

"Thank you, honey."

"Let's start right now. We'll be finished in
no time."

Grandma held Tanya close and patted her head. "It's gonna take quite a while to make this quilt, not a couple of days or a week—not even a month. A good quilt, a masterpiece..." Grandma's eyes shone at the thought. "Why I need more material. More gold and blue, some red and green. And I'll need the time to do it right. It'll take me a year at least."

"A year," shouted Tanya. "That's too long. I can't wait that long, Grandma."

Grandma laughed. "A year ain't that long, honey. Makin' this quilt gonna be a joy. Now run along and let Grandma rest." Grandma turned her head toward the sunlight and closed her eyes.

"I'm gonna make a masterpiece," she murmured, clutching a scrap of cloth in her hand, just before she fell asleep.

"We'll have to get you a new pair and use these old ones for rags," Mama said as she hung the last piece of wash on the clothesline one August afternoon.

Jim was miserable. His favorite blue corduroy pants had been held together with patches; now they were beyond repair.

"Bring them here," Grandma said.

Grandma took part of the pant leg and cut a few blue squares. Jim gave her a hug and watched her add his patches to the others.

"A quilt won't forget. It can tell your life story," she said.

The arrival of autumn meant school and Halloween. This year Tanya would be an African princess. She danced around in the long, flowing robes Mama had made from several yards of colorful material. The old bracelets and earrings Tanya had found in a trunk in the attic jingled noisily as she moved. Grandma cut some squares out of the leftover scraps and added Tanya to the quilt too!

The days grew colder but Tanya and her brothers didn't mind. They knew snow wasn't far away. Mama dreaded winter's coming. Every year she would plead with Grandma to move away from the drafty window, but Grandma wouldn't budge.

"Grandma, please," Mama scolded. "You can sit here by the heater."

"I'm not your grandmother, I'm your mother," Grandma said. "And I'm gonna sit here in the Lord's light and make my masterpiece."

It was the end of November when Ted, Jim, and Tanya got their wish. They awoke one morning to find everything in sight covered with snow. Tanya got dressed and flew down the stairs. Ted and Jim, and even Mama and Papa, were already outside.

"I don't like leaving Grandma in that house by herself," Mama said. "I know she's lonely."

Tanya pulled herself out of the snow being careful not to ruin her angel. "Grandma isn't lonely," Tanya said happily. "She and the quilt are telling each other stories."

Mama glanced questioningly at Tanya, "Telling each other stories?"

"Yes, Grandma says a quilt never forgets!"

The family spent the morning and most of the afternoon sledding down the hill. Finally, when they were all numb from the cold, they went inside for hot chocolate and sandwiches.

"I think I'll go sit and talk to Grandma," Mama said.

"Then she can explain to you about our quilt—our very own family quilt," Tanya said.

Mama saw the mischievous glint in her youngest child's eyes.

"Why, I may just have her do that, young lady," Mama said as she walked out of the kitchen.

Tanya leaned over the table to see into the living room. Grandma was hunched over, her eyes close to the fabric as she made tiny stitches. Mama sat at the old woman's feet. Tanya couldn't hear what was said but she knew Grandma was telling Mama all about quilts and how *this* quilt would be very special. Tanya sipped her chocolate slowly, then she saw Mama pick up a piece of fabric, rub it with her fingers, and smile.

From that moment on both women spent their winter evenings working on the quilt. Mama did the sewing while Grandma cut the fabrics and placed the scraps in a pattern of colors. Even while they were cooking and baking all their Christmas specialties during the day, at night they still worked on the quilt. Only once did Mama put it aside. She wanted to wear something special Christmas night, so she bought some gold material and made a beautiful dress. Tanya knew without asking that the gold scraps would be in the quilt too.

There was much singing and laughing that Christmas. All Grandma's sons and daughters and nieces and nephews came to pay their respects. The Christmas tree lights shone brightly, filling the room with sparkling colors. Later, when everyone had gone home, Papa said he had never felt so much happiness in the house. And Mama agreed.

When Tanya got downstairs the next morning, she found Papa fixing pancakes.

"Is today a special day too?" asked Jim.

"Where's Mama?" asked Tanya.

"Grandma doesn't feel well this morning," Papa said. "Your mother is with her now till the doctor gets here."

"Will Grandma be all right?" Ted asked.

Papa rubbed his son's head and smiled. "There's nothing for you to worry about. We'll take care of Grandma."

Tanya looked into the living room. There on the back of the big chair rested the patchwork quilt. It was folded neatly, just as Grandma had left it.

"Mother didn't want us to know she wasn't feeling well. She thought it would spoil our Christmas," Mama told them later, her face drawn and tired, her eyes a puffy red. "Now it's up to all of us to be quiet and make her as comfortable as possible." Papa put an arm around Mama's shoulder.

"Can we see Grandma?" Tanya asked.

"No, not tonight," Papa said. "Grandma needs plenty of rest."

It was nearly a week, the day before New Year's, before the children were permitted to see their grandmother. She looked tired and spoke in whispers.

"We miss you, Grandma," Ted said.

"And your muffins and hot chocolate," added Jim. Grandma smiled.

"Your quilt misses you too, Grandma," Tanya said. Grandma's smile faded from her lips. Her eyes grew cloudy.

"My masterpiece," Grandma sighed. "It would have been beautiful. Almost half finished." The old woman closed her eyes and turned away from her grandchildren. Papa whispered it was time to leave. Ted, Jim, and Tanya crept from the room.

Tanya walked slowly to where the quilt lay. She had seen Grandma and Mama work on it. Tanya thought real hard. She knew how to cut the scraps, but she wasn't certain of the rest. Just then Tanya felt a hand resting on her shoulder. She looked up and saw Mama.

"Tomorrow," Mama said.

New Year's Day was the beginning. After the dishes were washed and put away, Tanya and Mama examined the quilt.

"You cut more squares, Tanya, while I stitch some patches together," Mama said.

Tanya snipped and trimmed the scraps of material till her hands hurt from the scissors. Mama watched her carefully, making sure the squares were all the same size. The next day was the same as the last. More snipping and cutting. But Mama couldn't always be around to watch Tanya work. Grandma had to be looked after. So Tanya worked by herself. Then one night, as Papa read them stories, Jim walked over and looked at the quilt. In it he saw patches of blue. His blue. Without saying a word Jim picked up the scissors and some scraps and started to make squares. Ted helped Jim put the squares in piles while Mama showed Tanya how to join them.

Every day, as soon as she got home from school, Tanya worked on the quilt. Ted and Jim were too busy with sports, and Mama was looking after Grandma, so Tanya worked alone.

But after a few weeks she stopped. Something was wrong—something was missing, Tanya thought. For days the quilt lay on the back of the chair. No one knew why Tanya had stopped working. Tanya would sit and look at the quilt. Finally she knew. Some*thing* wasn't missing. Some*one* was missing from the quilt.

That evening before she went to bed Tanya tiptoed into Grandma's room, a pair of scissors in her hand. She quietly lifted the end of Grandma's old quilt and carefully removed a few squares.

February and March came and went as Mama proudly watched her daughter work on the last few rows of patches. Tanya always found time for the quilt. Grandma had been watching too. The old woman had been getting stronger and stronger as the months passed. Once she was able, Papa would carry Grandma to her chair by the window. "I needs the Lord's light," Grandma said. Then she would sit and hum softly to herself and watch Tanya work.

"Yes, honey, this quilt is nothin' but a joy," Grandma said.

Summer vacation was almost here. One June day Tanya came home to find Grandma working on the quilt again! She had finished sewing the last few squares together; the stuffing was in place, and she was already pinning on the backing.

"Grandma!" Tanya shouted.

Grandma looked up. "Hush, child. It's almost time to do the quilting on these patches. But first I have some special finishing touches...."

The next night Grandma cut the final thread with her teeth. "There. It's done," she said. Mama helped Grandma spread the quilt full length.

Nobody had realized how big it had gotten or how beautiful. Reds, greens, blues, and golds, light shades and dark, blended in and out throughout the quilt.

"It's beautiful," Papa said. He touched the gold patch, looked at Mama, and remembered. Jim remembered too. There was his blue and the red from Ted's shirt. There was Tanya's Halloween costume. And there was Grandma. Even though her patch was old, it fit right in.

They all remembered the past year. They especially remembered Tanya and all her work. So it had been decided. In the right hand corner of the last row of patches was delicately stitched, "For Tanya from your Mama and Grandma."

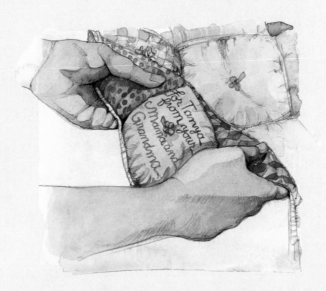

Reader's Response ～ What events in your life would you want to remember in a quilt?

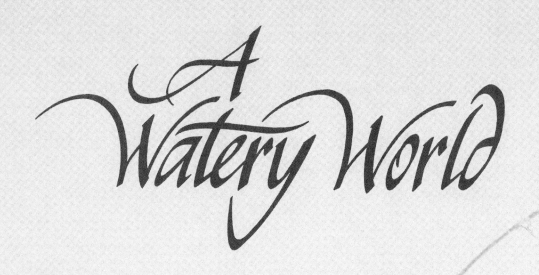

A Watery World

Many tales have been told about the seven seas.

What adventures await us in these watery worlds?

FISH IN WATER, *contemporary Chinese watercolor on silk*

A Watery World

*F*ind a place with water, and dream. Why
does a watery world capture our imagination?

❖ On Patricia's birthday, Dad
suggests visiting Clay Pit
Bottoms—the scariest place on
earth. What lurks beneath the Clay
Pit's murky waters? In *Some
Birthday!* by Patricia Polacco,
you'll read about the funniest,
scariest night of Patricia's life!

❖ Evil pirates, a brave boy, and an exciting sea adventure await you in the myth *Why Dolphins Call* by Jamie and Scott Simons. What will happen when Dionysus, one of the great Greek gods, is kidnapped by a band of pirates?

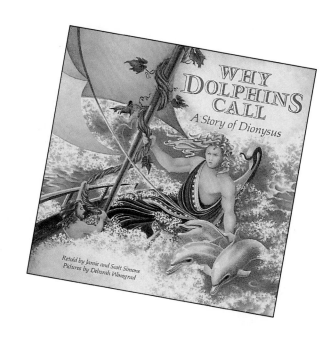

More Books to Enjoy

Skimmers by Downs Matthews
Life on a Fishing Boat by Huck Scarry
A First Look at Seashells by Millicent E. Selsam
    and Joyce Hunt
Sea Songs by Myra Cohn Livingston

Tim
to the Rescue

written and illustrated
by Edward Ardizzone

Little Tim was in his house by the sea. It was
stormy weather and Tim who was tired of his books
and lessons was looking out of the window and was
wishing that he was at sea again and having
tremendous adventures on some ship tossing about
among the waves.

But Tim had promised his parents to stay at
home and work hard and a promise like this has to
be kept.

"Oh dear," said Tim to himself. "I am bored with
my sums but I suppose I must learn them if I am to
become a real grown up sailor." Suddenly there was
a knock at the door. It was Tim's great friend
Captain McFee the old sea captain.

SEA
VIEW

"Fine news my boy," said McFee. "I am tired of being a landlubber so I have got a ship again. The S.S. Fidelity of 3000 Tons."

Tim longed more than anything else to go to sea with the captain and he begged his mother and father to let him go.

At last, as he had been a good boy and had worked hard at his lessons, they agreed, but said that he could go for one voyage only, and that he must promise to work at his lesson books in his spare time.

Captain McFee was pleased. He would take Tim as second ship's boy, but he warned Tim that once on board they could not be the same sort of friends as before. On board he was the skipper and discipline must be maintained.

"Aye Aye Sir," said Tim.

Soon the great day for leaving arrived. Tim's
father and mother came to see him off. His mother
cried a little when he waved goodbye. Tim could
not help feeling rather sad and lonely too.

The first person Tim met on board was a tall
red haired boy called Ginger.

"Blimey," said Ginger. "What's 'ere? A blooming
passenger or is it the new third mate?" This made
Tim cross but he answered politely that he was the
second ship's boy.

"Second ship's boy," said Ginger. "Well I am first ship's boy, so you will jolly well have to do what I tell you or I will bash you. I've a good mind to bash you now just to teach you." However, as Tim did not move and did not seem afraid, Ginger became quite nice. He showed Tim the cabin they were to share and took him to see the Bosun. On the way he warned Tim to avoid the captain as he was a regular Tartar. Knowing Captain McFee Tim could not help feeling surprised, but perhaps people change when they go on board a ship. Would he become a Tartar too?

The Bosun seemed quite kind and said to Tim, "Do what you are told and look slippy about it and you will be all right."

"Aye Aye," said Tim smartly.

Soon the ship started. Tim and Ginger leant on the rail and watched as they moved slowly down the wide river to the open sea.

Once at sea Tim was kept busy doing odd jobs. But when the weather was fine and he had no duties to do, he would sit on deck in some sunny spot and study hard.

Soon he had the reputation of being a scholar.

He gave lessons in—

<u>READING & WRITING</u> to Ginger who was very backward. <u>ARITHMETIC</u> to Fireman Jones who wanted to become an engineer. <u>HISTORY</u> to Alaska Pete who had a passion for King Charles I and wanted to know all about him. In the evening Tim wrote letters for old Joe the cook who could not read or write at all.

Ginger I am sorry to say was a lazy and mischievous boy. Instead of working he would hide in some corner and look at comics. When he was hungry he would steal the seamen's marmalade, and when he wished to amuse himself he teased the ship's cat which made Tim very cross because he liked cats. Now Ginger's worst mischief was to have the most terrible results for him.

The Third Mate was very bald and rather vain. He had in his cabin many bottles filled with different coloured hair growers.

One day Ginger went to his cabin with a message and finding he was out could not resist trying all the bottles on his head.

The last bottle that Ginger tried had a very curious shape and was full of a strange smelling green liquid.

When he put it on his head it gave him a lovely tingly feeling.

Poor Ginger! Little did he know what was happening. His hair was growing and growing and GROWING.

"Crikey," said Tim when he met Ginger on the deck. "Go and get your hair cut before the captain sees you."

Ginger had his hair cut, but alas to no avail.

In one hour's time it was like this.

In two
hour's time like this,

and soon it would have become like this if the captain had not seen him. "Bosun," roared Captain McFee, "get that boy's hair cut."

From now on Ginger had a terrible time. Everybody who saw him shouted, "Go and get your hair cut" until he was almost in tears of dismay.

Alaska Pete and Joe the cook spent so much time making horrid mixtures to stop his hair growing [the mixtures never did] that they neglected the cooking, which made the crew very cross.

Seaman Bloggs the ship's barber said that he was sick and tired of it, that his fingers were worn to the bone and that he ought to have extra pay.

In fact the ship was going to the dogs.

Ginger became so unhappy that he took to hiding in the boats. His only friends were Tim and the ship's cat, which says a lot for cats considering how nasty Ginger had been to it.

Tim would visit Ginger as often as he could and would bring him his dinner and cut his hair with a large pair of scissors that he had borrowed from Seaman Bloggs.

And so things went on from bad to worse. One day the sky became cloudy and the sea had an oily swell. The crew grumbled about the food. The bosun was worried and the new mixture that Pete and Joe were making smelt so horribly that even the ship's cat was put off his dinner.

Tim was standing on the bridge when he heard Captain McFee say to the Mate, "What do you think of the weather Mr. Mate? I don't like it a bit.

There is a hurricane blowing up or I'll eat my hat. Order all hands on deck to batten down hatches and see that the ship's boys keep below."

The next few hours were busy ones for the crew making everything secure and shipshape on the decks. By now the wind was blowing great guns and the waves were getting bigger and bigger, occasionally dashing over the side and wetting the crew with spray. But where was Ginger all this time? Still hiding in the boat.

Tim had tried hard to make him come below but he just would not.

In the meantime Tim was sitting with old Joe in the galley. He was terribly worried about Ginger thinking how cold and hungry he must be up there in the great gale.

Finally, orders or no orders, he decided to go to him once more and try and persuade him to come down. Tim crept up the companionway and with great difficulty pushed open the door onto the deck.

What he saw there made him very frightened. The sky was black with flying cloud, the wind was shrieking and great waves towered up on every side as if at any moment they would swamp the ship.

Standing there the thought came to him that Ginger must be saved. He must somehow get to him and force him to come below.

Tim waited for a moment until he thought it was a little calmer, then he dashed across the deck; but half way there a great wave came overboard and nearly swept him away. He just managed to save himself and reach the boat.

Inside the boat was Ginger. He was cold, wet and frightened and was holding the ship's cat in his arms. "Come below with me," shouted Tim again and again; but the wild wind only blew his words away.

At last Ginger heard. "No!" he cried. "I can't, I am too frightened." Nothing that Tim could do or say would make him move, so Tim left him to go back and get the crew to help.

He had only gone a short way on his dangerous homeward journey when a tremendous wave rushed down upon him. He leapt for the rigging and then looked round. There was no boat, no Ginger, and no cat.

Tim was horrified. "Poor Ginger, poor puss," he thought. Then in the backwash of the wave he saw the half drowned cat.

Quickly he pulled it out of the water and put it in the rigging.

Next he saw a great red mop of hair floating by. It was Ginger's. He grabbed it and hung on. He thought his arm would break, so hard did the rushing water try to tug Ginger away.

Captain McFee had seen them. "All hands to the rescue," he shouted.

Alaska Pete and Old Joe tied themselves to ropes and with tremendous courage dashed across the deck and soon had carried all three of them back to safety.

The Captain seemed furious. "How dare you disobey my orders and be on deck?" he said to Tim and Ginger. "Go below at once and if I catch you on deck again I will have you both beaten with a rope's end."

"Bosun," he roared. "Get that boy's HAIR CUT."

However, as they left to go Tim saw the Captain brush a tear from his eye and heard him say:

"Drat those boys Mr. Mate, wouldn't lose them for the world. Fine boy Tim. Fine boy."

Once below Pete and Joe wrapped them in blankets and put them to bed.

Seaman Bloggs cut Ginger's hair while Joe gave them mugs of hot cocoa, and a dish of warm milk to the cat.

Alaska Pete insisted on taking their temperatures and dosing them with some very nasty medicine to prevent them getting chills. Soon they were all asleep.

Tim woke up feeling very well. He looked at Ginger and had a great surprise. Ginger's hair had not grown at all.

"Are you well Ginger?" Tim said. "Yes, fine," answered Ginger. "Well look at yourself in the glass," said Tim. You can just imagine how pleased and surprised Ginger was to see his nice short hair.

Now, curious to tell, perhaps it was the cold sea water, perhaps it was the shock; but from this time on Ginger's hair grew in the ordinary slow way. In a few days time the sun came out, the sea was calm, and the weather became warm and fine.

Tim and Ginger were back at their usual jobs, the crew were busy hanging out their clothes to dry, when the captain ordered all hands to the forward well deck.

There he made a speech from the bridge.

"Men," he said, "during the storm the two ship's boys disobeyed my orders and nearly got drowned.

However, now that I have heard the full story I realise that ship's boy Tim only went on deck to rescue his companion Ginger. It was a very gallant action and I am going to ask the Royal Humane Society to give him a gold medal."—Cheers from the crew—"Alaska Pete and Old Joe," the Captain continued, "were very brave to face the raging sea and rescue the two boys and the cat. I will give them each £5"—Loud cheers—"But I hope that in the future they will both give up making nasty smelling mixtures and get on with the cooking"—Prolonged cheers. As you can imagine after this Tim was very popular with everyone. Ginger was a reformed character. He worked well and became quite popular too.

Joe and Pete were their special friends. In the evening when the day's work was done they would sit together and tell stories. Tim thrilled them all with tales of how he was shipwrecked and of Mr. Grimes and the mutineers. Joe was so impressed that he always called Tim the little skipper.

From now on too the Bosun took a special interest in Tim and spent much time teaching him many things that a sailor should know. Tim would repeat the lessons to Ginger who became quite clever.

But with all this you must not think that Tim neglected his lesson books, because he did not.

After a long and happy voyage the ship came back to port. Tim's Mother and Father were on the dock to meet him. They invited Ginger to stay with them which he was very pleased to do as he had no home of his own.

Tim went back to school and Ginger went with him. Tim was first in class for Reading, Writing, Arithmetic, History, and Geography, which just goes to show how hard he had worked at his books.

Ginger was second in Geography, which showed that he had worked hard too.

But Tim's proudest moment came when there arrived by post a beautiful gold medal and a roll of parchment on which was written the story of his brave adventure. Tim's father had the roll framed and hung it in the drawing room.

∽ THE END ∽

Reader's Response ∽ Do you think Tim did the right thing when he disobeyed the Captain and looked for Ginger?

Library Link ∽ *If you liked this story by Edward Ardizzone, you might enjoy reading some of his other books, such as* Little Tim and the Brave Sea Captain *and* Tim and Charlotte.

The Gulf Stream

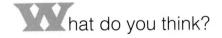

The Gulf Stream by Winslow Homer, 1899

Winslow Homer was an American artist who loved to paint stories about the sea.

The Gulf Stream shows a fisherman shipwrecked during a storm. When someone complained that the painting was too scary, Winslow Homer wrote that the fisherman "will be rescued and returned to his friends and home, and ever after live happily."

What do you think?

Until I Saw
the Sea

Until I saw the sea
I did not know
that wind
could wrinkle water so.

I never knew
that sun
could splinter a whole sea of blue.

Nor
did I know before,
a sea breathes in and out
upon a shore.

Lilian Moore

97

The Sea of Gold

by Yoshiko Uchida

On a small island, where almost every able-bodied man was a fisherman, there once lived a young man named Hikoichi. He was gentle and kind, but he was not very bright, and there was no one on the whole island who was willing to teach him how to become a fisherman.

"How could we ever make a fisherman out of you?" people would say to him. "You are much too slow to learn anything!"

99

But Hikoichi wanted very badly to go to work, and he tried hard to find a job. He looked and looked for many months until finally he found work as cook on one of the fishing boats. He got the job, however, only because no one else wanted it. No one wanted to work in a hot steaming galley, cooking rice and chopping vegetables, while the boat pitched and rolled in the middle of the sea. No one wanted to be the cook who always got the smallest share of the boat's catch.

But Hikoichi didn't mind at all. He was happy to have any kind of job at last.

The fishermen on his boat liked to tease him and they would often call him Slowpoke or Stupid. "Get busy and make us something decent to eat, Stupid!" they would shout to him. Or, "The rice is only half-cooked, Slowpoke!" they would complain.

But no matter how they shouted or what they called him, Hikoichi never grew angry. He only answered, "Yes sir," or "I'm sorry, sir," and that was all.

Hikoichi was very careful with the food he cooked, and he tried not to waste even a single grain of rice. In fact, he hated to throw away any of the leftovers, and he stored them carefully in the galley cupboards. On the small, crowded fishing vessel, however, there was no room for keeping useless things. Every bit of extra space was needed to store the catch, for the more fish they took back to the island, the more money they would all make. When the men discovered that Hikoichi was saving the leftovers, they scolded him harshly.

"Stupid fool!" they shouted. "Don't use our valuable space for storing garbage. Throw it into the sea!"

"What a terrible waste of good food," Hikoichi thought, but he had to do as he was told. He gathered up all the leftovers he had stored and took them up on deck.

"If I must throw this into the sea," he said to himself, "I will make sure the fish have a good feast. After all, if it were not for the fish, we wouldn't be able to make a living." And so, as he threw the leftovers into the water, he called out, "Here fish, here, good fish, have yourselves a splendid dinner!"

From that day, Hikoichi always called to the fish before he threw his leftovers into the sea. "*Sah sah*, come along," he would call. "Enjoy some rice from my galley!" And he continued talking to them until they had devoured every morsel he tossed overboard.

The fishermen laughed when they heard him. "Listen to the young fool talking to the fish," they jeered. And to Hikoichi they said, "Maybe someday they will answer you and tell you how much they enjoyed your dinner."

But Hikoichi didn't pay any attention to the fishermen. He silently gathered all the scraps from the table and continued to toss them out to the fish at the end of the day. Each time he did, he called to the fish as though they were his best friends, and his gentle voice echoed far out over the dancing waves of the sea.

In such a fashion, many years went by until Hikoichi was no longer a young man. He continued to cook for the men on his fishing boat, however, and he still fed and talked to the fish every evening.

One day, the fishing boat put far out to sea in search of bigger fish. It sailed for three days and three nights, going farther and farther away from the small island. On the third night, they were still far out at sea when they dropped anchor. It was a quiet star-filled night with a full moon glowing high in the sky. The men were tired from the day's work and not long after dinner, they were all sound asleep.

Hikoichi, however, still had much to do. He scrubbed the pots, cleaned up his galley and washed the rice for breakfast. When he had finished, he gathered all the leftovers in a basket and went up on deck.

"Gather around, good fish," he called as always. "Enjoy your dinner."

He emptied his basket and stayed to watch the fish eat up his food. Then, he went to his bunk to prepare for bed, but somehow the boat felt very peculiar.

It had stopped rolling. In fact, it was not moving
at all and felt as though it were standing on
dry land.

"That's odd," Hikoichi thought, and he ran up
on deck to see what had happened. He leaned over
the rail and looked out.

"What!" he shouted. "The ocean is gone!"

And indeed it had disappeared. There was
not a single drop of water anywhere. As far as
Hikoichi could see, there was nothing but miles
and miles of sand. It was as though the boat
were standing in the middle of a vast desert of
shimmering sand.

"What has happened?" Hikoichi wondered.
"Have we suddenly beached ourselves on an
unknown island? Did the ocean dry up? But no,
that is impossible. I must be dreaming!"

Hikoichi blinked hard and shook his head.
Then he pinched himself on the cheek, but he was
not dreaming. Hikoichi was alarmed. He wanted
to go below to wake the others, but he knew they
would be very angry to be awakened in the middle
of the night. They would shout at him and call him
a stupid fool and tell him he was out of his mind.
Hikoichi decided he wouldn't awaken them after
all. If the boat was still on land in the morning, the
men would see for themselves.

Hikoichi could not believe his eyes. He simply had to get off the boat to see if they really were standing on dry land. Slowly, he lowered himself down a rope ladder and reached the sand below. Carefully, he took a step and felt his foot crunch on something solid. No, it wasn't water. It really was sand after all. Hikoichi blinked as he looked around, for under the light of the moon, the sand glittered and sparkled like a beach of gold. He scooped up a handful and watched it glisten as it slid through his fingers.

"Why, this is beautiful," Hikoichi thought, and his heart sang with joy at the splendor of the sight. "I must save some of this sand so I can remember this wonderful night forever." He hurried back onto the boat for a bucket, filled it with the sparkling sand and then carried it aboard and hid it carefully beneath his bunk. He looked around at the other men, but they were all sound asleep. Not one seemed to have noticed that the boat was standing still. Hikoichi slipped quietly into his narrow, dark bunk, and soon he too was sound asleep.

The next morning Hikoichi was the first to wake up. He remembered the remarkable happening of the night before, and he leaped out of bed, ready to call the other men to see the strange sight. But as he got dressed, he felt the familiar rocking of the boat. He hurried up on deck and he saw that once again they were out in the middle of the ocean with waves all about them. Hikoichi shook his head, but now he could no longer keep it all to himself. As soon as the other men came up on deck, he told his story.

"It's true," he cried as he saw wide grins appear on the men's faces. "The ocean was gone and for miles and miles there was nothing but sand. It glittered and sparkled under the full moon and it was as though we were sailing on a sea of golden sand!"

The men roared with laughter. "Hikoichi, you were surely drunk," they said. "Now, put away your daydreams and fix us some breakfast."

"No, no, I wasn't drunk and I wasn't dreaming," Hikoichi insisted. "I climbed down the ladder and I walked on the sand. I picked it up and felt it slip through my fingers. It wasn't a dream. It really wasn't."

"Poor old Slowpoke," the men sneered. "Your brain has finally become addled. We will have to send you home."

It was then that Hikoichi remembered his bucket. "Wait! Come with me and I can prove it," he said, and he led the men down to his bunk. Then, getting down on his hands and knees, he carefully pulled out his bucket of sand.

"There!" he said proudly. "I scooped this up when I went down and walked on the sand. Now do you believe me?"

The men suddenly stopped laughing. "This isn't sand," they said, reaching out to feel it. "It's gold! It's a bucket full of pure gold!"

"Why didn't you get more, you poor fool?" one of the men shouted.

"You've got to give some of it to us," another added.

"We share our fish with you. You must share your gold with us," said still another.

Soon all the men were yelling and shouting and pushing to get their hands on Hikoichi's bucket of gold.

Then the oldest of the fishermen spoke up. "Stop it! Stop it!" he called out. "This gold doesn't belong to any of you. It belongs to Hikoichi."

He reminded the men how Hikoichi had fed the fish of the sea for so many years as though they were his own children.

"Now the King of the Sea has given Hikoichi a reward for his kindness to the fish," he explained. And turning to Hikoichi, he added, "You are not stupid or a fool or a slowpoke, my friend. You are gentle and kind and good. This gift from the Kingdom of the Sea is your reward. Take all the gold and keep it, for it belongs only to you."

The shouting, pushing fishermen suddenly became silent and thoughtful, for they knew the old fisherman was right. They were ashamed of having laughed at Hikoichi year after year, and they knew that he truly deserved this fine reward.

Without another word the men went back to work. They completed their catch that day and the heavily laden boat returned once more to the little island.

The next time the boat put out to sea, Hikoichi was no longer aboard, for now he had enough gold to leave his job as cook forever. He built himself a beautiful new house, and he even had a small boat of his own so he could still sail out to sea and feed the fish. He used his treasure from the sea wisely and well, and he lived a long and happy life on the little island where no one ever called him Stupid or Slowpoke again.

Reader's Response   What did you think of Hikoichi? Would you like him to be your friend? Why or why not?

Meet
Yoshiko Uchida

Yoshiko Uchida began writing stories when she was ten years old. She wrote them on brown wrapping paper, which she cut up and bound into books.

Ms. Uchida also kept a journal when she was young. She still liked to read it as an adult to remember important times—like the day she got her first dog. "By putting these special happenings into words and writing them down, I was trying to hold on to and somehow preserve the magic as well as the joy and sadness of the moments. . . . I guess that's what books and writing are all about."

This is Yoshiko Uchida as a ten-year-old girl.

The Wonderful Underwater Machine

by Josephine Edgar

A team of engineers and scientists at the Woods Hole Oceanographic Institution in Massachusetts wanted to study the deepest parts of the ocean. They knew it was impossible for people to survive outside a submarine in the deepest parts of the ocean, so the team worked together to build a machine called Jason Jr., or "JJ" for short.

If you saw Jason Jr. swimming at the bottom of the ocean, you might think you were looking at a big, blue bug with two bright eyes. But JJ is not a bug, and its bright eyes are really two bright lights! JJ is a small machine, only twenty-eight inches long, but it is capable of swimming deep in the ocean.

Deep under the ocean, the weight of the water pushes down very hard on anything found on the ocean floor. Sometimes there are sharp rocks and coral that can harm and even tear apart a machine. So the engineers knew they had to make JJ strong. The engineers could not make all of JJ's parts out of metal though, because a heavy metal machine would sink to the bottom of the ocean. They solved this problem by making a special skin for JJ.

The outside of JJ's skin is made of blue fiberglass. The fiberglass covers millions of tiny glass balls. These balls are smaller than grains of sand, and each ball has air inside, like a tiny bubble. The balls are glued together and help JJ float in the water. The tiny glass balls are also hard like marbles. When JJ bumps into something sharp, the balls protect it.

This is Jason Jr., also referred to as JJ. If you saw JJ in the water, what would you think it was?

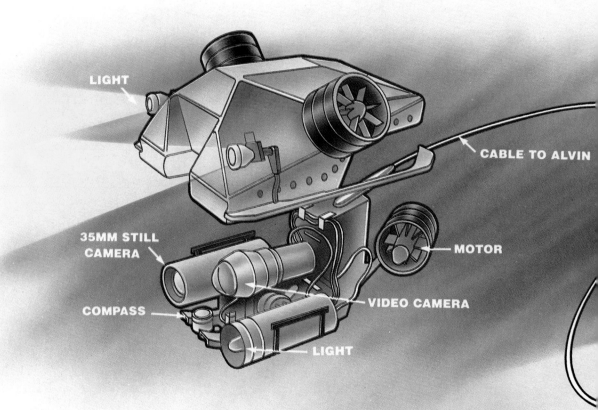

LIGHT

CABLE TO ALVIN

35MM STILL
CAMERA

MOTOR

COMPASS

VIDEO CAMERA

LIGHT

JJ's protective cover has been lifted so you can see how it looks inside.

Inside JJ are motors that help it move and two cameras that take pictures of what it sees.

Behind JJ is a long cable that looks like a tail. This cable is more than 200 feet long. Because it's bendable, JJ can swim in any direction. The cable is also very strong, and it keeps the wires inside it safe and dry. These wires are very important, because the scientists use them to send signals to JJ that tell the machine what to do. The wires also send television pictures and signals back to the scientists. The signals tell what JJ finds.

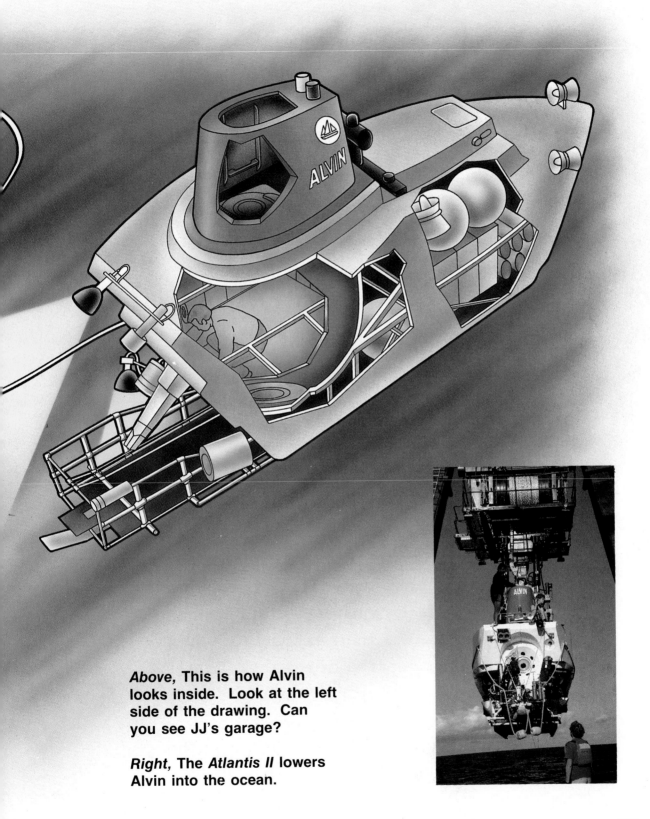

Above, This is how Alvin
looks inside. Look at the left
side of the drawing. Can
you see JJ's garage?

Right, The *Atlantis II* lowers
Alvin into the ocean.

Atlantis II stands by while Alvin takes JJ down to the ocean bottom to explore and to take pictures.

To get to the bottom of the ocean, Jason Jr. gets a ride from Alvin. Alvin is a submarine that can dive in very deep water. It carries JJ in a small garage, which is just under the front window. Inside Alvin there is room for two scientists and a pilot who drives the submarine.

The scientists use a big ship named *Atlantis II* to take Alvin and JJ out into the ocean. Then, *Atlantis II* lowers Alvin into the water, and the submarine starts to go down.

Alvin drops quickly because the scientists have put heavy steel weights on Alvin to make it sink. In one minute, Alvin can fall 100 feet. As Alvin goes down, the water gets darker and darker. First the ocean is blue. Then it is dark blue. In fifteen minutes, it is so dark that the scientists must turn on the lights inside Alvin to see. It is dark because sunlight can't reach the deepest parts of the ocean.

The scientists can't see the bottom, but they can tell when they are getting close to it by using Alvin's sonar. The sonar machine makes a noise and listens for the noise to bounce off the ocean floor. When the scientists hear the echo a short time after the noise is made, they know that the ocean floor is close.

Alvin's sonar tells scientists how close it is to the ocean bottom. This diagram shows how sonar works.

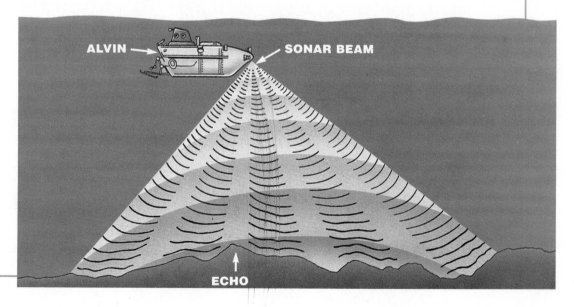

When they are near to the bottom, the scientists drop one of Alvin's heavy weights. This makes Alvin slow down. Then, as they let go of more weights, Alvin settles down softly in the mud at the bottom. Using Alvin's lights, the scientists can see out of the small windows. Now, they are ready to use Jason Jr., to get a closer look.

Next, JJ swims out pulling its cable behind it. The scientists signal JJ where to look. It shines its lights on whatever the scientists are studying and takes pictures. JJ sends the pictures back to the scientists through the cable, which is also attached to Alvin.

The scientists are using JJ to look closely at rocks and mountains in the deepest parts of the ocean. They are learning where we can find important metals. They are also using JJ to study fish and other living things. JJ's pictures help the scientists understand how we can use the oceans to raise fish and other food.

After JJ has been on the ocean bottom for almost four hours, the scientists signal it to come back to Alvin. It is time to go home. Alvin comes back up to return to *Atlantis II.*

The next day the scientists will take Alvin and JJ down again. They are eager to find out more about what lies beneath the ocean.

In 1986 the scientists from the Woods Hole Oceanographic Institution used JJ to explore a famous ship that sank to the bottom of the ocean many years ago. In 1912 this large ship hit an iceberg and sank. The ship was the *Titanic.*

The scientists wanted to test JJ to find out how well it could swim inside the ship and take pictures. JJ did very well. It even swam down stairs and looked into rooms. The scientists sitting inside Alvin could see the pictures that JJ sent back. The pictures showed ceiling lamps and an old, rusty bathtub, but all the wooden furniture and stairs were gone. The scientists guessed that small shellfish had eaten anything wooden. The pictures also showed cups and bottles resting on the ocean bottom next to the shipwreck.

JJ approaches the sunken *Titanic*. Scientists were able to see the inside of the ship from the pictures JJ took.

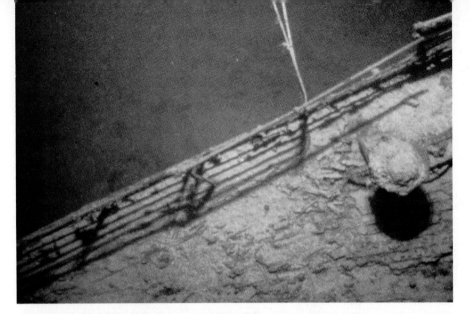

JJ took this photograph of the *Titanic's* deck. How can you tell the ship has been underwater for a long time?

Engineers at Woods Hole are now building newer and bigger machines like Jason Jr. and Alvin. Some of these machines will help them make better maps of the mountains and valleys on the ocean floor. Others will give us closer looks at shipwrecks. The underwater machines of the future will help scientists learn more about our oceans so that we can use them safely and wisely.

Reader's Response ∿ If you wanted to tell your friends about Alvin and JJ, what would you say?

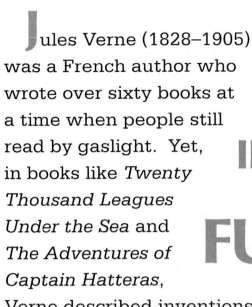

THE MAN WHO INVENTED THE FUTURE

Jules Verne (1828–1905) was a French author who wrote over sixty books at a time when people still read by gaslight. Yet, in books like *Twenty Thousand Leagues Under the Sea* and *The Adventures of Captain Hatteras*, Verne described inventions and adventures undreamed of by readers of his day.

diving suits
television
a submarine called the *Nautilus*
airplanes   space rockets
underwater exploration
a trip to the moon

Many of Verne's fictional inventions have come true. Some are still waiting to be invented: a world capital with rolling sidewalks; advertising on clouds; and a car-boat-plane that can go everywhere! Maybe you can use one of these ideas to invent the future.

121

Turtle Watch

from the
book written
and photographed
by **George Ancona**

The number of sea turtles nesting along the beaches of Brazil gets smaller every year. People are worried! If this keeps happening, the sea turtles will disappear forever. In the small beach town of Praia do Forte the government has set up a special project to protect the turtles. Its name is TAMAR and it is run by three scientists, Neca, Guy, and Alexandre.

Sea turtles nest along beaches of tropical and subtropical lands. In the Western Hemisphere, these include the beaches of North, Central, and South America and the islands of the Caribbean.

The threat to turtles nesting here has been so great that today six of the hemisphere's seven species of sea turtles are considered endangered.

Scientists and conservationists alone cannot save the sea turtles. The people who depend on turtles for their income must help. In the town of Praia do Forte, TAMAR has been working with the fishermen. Guy and Neca have hired those known to be good at finding eggs. The men have been adding to their income by taking eggs to TAMAR. Their children have been growing up with new ideas about turtles.

Two of these children, Flavio and Rosa, have always lived in Praia do Forte. Their father, Everaldo, is a fisherman who is very knowledgeable about turtles. He was one of the first men asked to find eggs for TAMAR.

Flavio and Rosa often roam the beach in their free time. They also like to visit their grandfather and hear about his life as a fisherman, about the time when there were plenty of turtle eggs to sell and eat. He tells the children how good the eggs tasted—and how he misses them.

Praia do Forte

After leaving their grandfather, the children go out to explore the beach for turtle nests. Flavio wears Grandfather's old hat. Most of the time the nests have been emptied by the oceanographers. But when Rosa sees the remains of a turtle's tracks, the children become excited. Perhaps this nest was made after the jeep finished its last tour of the night. They both begin to poke around in the sand.

Picking up a stick, Flavio and Rosa probe the sand the way their grandfather taught them. Sure enough, Rosa feels the stick slip into the egg cavity. They both begin to dig furiously, sending the sand flying in all directions.

Soon Flavio cannot reach any deeper, but Rosa, who is bigger, continues to dig. Stretching out her hand, she touches the leathery eggs and shouts with excitement.

Then she hands the eggs to Flavio, who places them very carefully inside Grandfather's hat. When the hat is full, the children decide to stop and cover the rest of the eggs.

After covering the nest and marking the spot, Rosa and Flavio run to show their father the eggs. Along the way, they are joined by friends.

When Rosa and Flavio call out to him, their father appears over the side of the boat he is repairing. Flavio holds out the egg-filled hat. Everaldo is pleased that his children are also skilled at finding eggs. He tells them to show Guy and Neca what they have found. The children leave for the lighthouse.

The lighthouse is only a little way up the beach from the fishing boats. The area around it is fenced off. Inside the fence are rows of buried eggs that were found on the beaches. Each nest is surrounded by a mesh fence. There are also three large, round tanks where captive turtles are raised for study. Palm fronds shelter the tanks from the hot tropical sun.

The children are glad to have an excuse to visit the project. And Neca is delighted to see them and to receive the eggs.

Neca takes Rosa and Flavio to the rows of buried eggs. With a posthole digger, she makes a new hole. Rosa sticks her arm out to show Neca how deep the eggs were.

Just as the turtle did, Neca widens the base of the hole. She places the eggs in their new nest and covers them with sand. Then she takes a metal screen and forms a fence around the eggs, burying half of the fence in the sand.

Rosa and Flavio offer to take Neca to the nest where the rest of the eggs are.

But before Neca can leave, she must note in a large book the number of eggs she has buried and the place where they were found. She must also assign the nest a number, which is painted on a stick and placed in the nest.

Flavio and Rosa climb into the back of the jeep. The children are thrilled to go for a ride. They bump along the coconut groves at the top of the beach until Rosa points out the site of the nest.

Once Neca has safely packed the rest of the eggs in a Styrofoam cooler and placed them in the jeep, she brings out a long white pole to mark the site of the empty nest. The pole has the same number as the one with the eggs she has buried—14.

Neca tells the children that the eggs will hatch in about fifty days. At that time they can come to see their hatchlings.

Fifty days seems like such a long time to wait. Flavio and Rosa now make regular visits to the turtle pens. Often they wait for their father and the other fishermen to return from fishing. Sometimes little silver fish get stuck in the fishermen's nets. When the men shake out their nets on the beach, the children collect the little fish that fall out. These they take to the turtles in the tanks. Soon they have the turtles coming up to be fed.

Almost every night, while Rosa and Flavio are sleeping, turtles are hatching. Deep within the egg cavity, baby turtles break through their shells and, working together, burrow their way up through the sand. Soon the first tiny hatchling reaches the surface. It is then joined by dozens of little brothers and sisters.

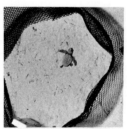

Turtles prefer to hatch in the cool of the night. They also enjoy the protection of the darkness, which hides them from predators.

During the day their tiny black bodies would dry up on the hot sand.

Now time is short. Once the hatchlings are out of their shells, they must hurry to the protective ocean. Neca and Alexandre count the hatchlings, record the number, and place them in a box.

Alexandre drives the hatchlings to the site of their original nest, which is marked by a white numbered pole. There he releases them onto the sand. He wants them to experience the same conditions they would have if they had hatched there. Like little windup toys, their tiny flippers flailing, the hatchlings climb over one another and begin to scramble toward the sea. They are attracted by the luminous waves of the ocean. Alexandre helps them by standing in the shallow water with a flashlight.

Soon the hatchlings reach the white foamy edge of the surf. As they scurry to the safety of the ocean, wave after wave carries them away. When the last little hatchling is swallowed up by the sea, all that is left of them are the tiny tracks on the beach.

It has been fifty-three days since Flavio and Rosa found their eggs. That night Neca sticks her hand inside the nest and feels some movement. Sure enough, later in the night the hatchlings of pen number 14 begin to emerge.

At dawn, Neca goes to fetch Flavio and Rosa. The children hurry to the pen to watch. As the little baby turtles squirm and climb over one another, the children giggle with glee.

Now the sun is getting higher in the sky, and the heat of the day is beginning. Neca says they must hurry. They work together to load the hatchlings into a Styrofoam cooler.

In no time, the jeep takes them to pole number 14, the site of their original nest. Neca puts the box on its side, and the hatchlings make their way instinctively toward the ocean.

Thanks to Rosa and Flavio, who protect them from the birds, all the hatchlings complete their journey—all but one. Rosa picks up this last straggler. Gently she puts it down closer to the water. With the next wave the sea covers her hand, and the last of Rosa and Flavio's hatchlings is gone.

Reader's Response ∿ If you could talk to Rosa and Flavio, what questions would you ask them?

Missing

Sea turtles have lived on our planet for about seventy million years. Today, they are in danger of disappearing forever. Where have the turtles gone?

Every few years female sea turtles leave the ocean several times to lay their eggs. Because salt water kills turtle eggs, the female turtles have to bury them where the ocean water can't reach them. Once on the beach, the slow-moving turtles are easy for turtle hunters to catch. These people eat and sell the turtles and their eggs, so they take as many as they can find.

What happens to the ones they sell? Restaurants use the turtles to make turtle soup and other turtle dishes. Other companies make turtle-shell eyeglass frames, jewelry, and barrettes; turtle-skin wallets and shoes; and turtle-oil skin care products. The eggs are packaged and sold as special treats.

It will take many years of careful conservation to make the turtles safe again.

The
Monkey
and the
CROCODILE

A Jataka Tale from India

written and illustrated by Paul Galdone

Beside a river in the jungle stood a tall mango tree. In the tree lived many monkeys. They swung from branch to branch, eating fruit and chattering to each other.

Hungry crocodiles swam in the river and sunned themselves on the banks.

One young crocodile was hungrier than all the rest. He could never get enough to eat.

The young crocodile watched the monkeys for a long time. Then one day he said to a wise old crocodile: "I'd like to catch a monkey and eat him!"

"How would you ever catch a monkey?" asked the old crocodile. "You do not travel on land and monkeys do not go into the water. Besides, they are quicker than you are."

"They may be quicker," said the young crocodile, "but I am more cunning. You will see!"

For days the crocodile swam back and forth, studying the monkeys all the while.

Then he noticed one young monkey who was quicker than all the others. This monkey loved to jump to the highest branches of the tree and pick the ripe mangos at the very top.

"He's the one I want," the crocodile said to himself. "But how am I going to catch him?"

The crocodile thought and thought, and at last he had an idea.

"Monkey," he called, "wouldn't you like to come with me over to the island, where the fruit is so ripe?"

"Oh, yes," said the monkey. "But how can I go with you? I do not swim."

"I will take you on my back," said the crocodile, with a toothy smile.

The monkey was eager to get to the fruit, so he jumped down on the crocodile's back.

"Off we go!" said the crocodile, gliding through the water.

"This is a fine ride you are giving me," said the monkey.

"Do you think so? Well, how do you like this?" asked the crocodile. And suddenly he dived down into the water.

"Oh, please don't!" cried the monkey as he went under. He was afraid to let go and he did not know what to do.

When the crocodile came up, the monkey sputtered and choked. "Why did you take me under water, Crocodile?" he asked. "You know I can't swim!"

"Because I am going to drown you," replied the crocodile. "And then I am going to eat you."

The monkey shivered in fear. But he thought quickly and before the crocodile dived again, he said: "I wish you had told me you wanted to eat me. If I had known that, I would have brought my heart."

"Your heart?" asked the crocodile.

"Yes, it is the tastiest part of me. But I left it behind in the tree."

"Then we must go back and get it," said the crocodile, turning around.

"But we are so near the island," said the monkey. "Please take me there first."

"No," said the crocodile. "First I am taking you straight to your tree. You will get your heart and bring it to me at once. Then we will see about going to the island."

"Very well," said the monkey.

And the crocodile headed back to the river bank.

No sooner did the monkey jump onto the bank than up he swung into the tree. From the highest branch he called down to the crocodile: "My heart is way up here. If you want it, come for it! Come for it!" And he laughed and laughed while the crocodile thrashed his tail in anger.

That night the monkey moved far down river from the mango tree. He wanted to get away from the crocodile so he could live in peace.

But the crocodile was still determined to catch him. He searched and searched and finally he found the monkey, living in another tree.

Here a large rock rose out of the water, halfway between the monkey's new home and the island. The crocodile watched the monkey jumping from the river bank to the rock, and then to the island where the fruit trees were.

"Monkey will stay on the island all day," the crocodile thought to himself. "And I'll catch him on his way home tonight."

The monkey had a fine feast, while the crocodile swam about, watching him all day. Toward night, the crocodile crawled out of the water and lay on the rock, perfectly still.

When it grew dark among the trees, the monkey started for home. He ran down to the river bank, and there he stopped.

"What is the matter with the rock?" the monkey wondered. "I never saw it so high before. Something must be lying on it."

The monkey went to the water's edge and called: "Hello, Rock!"

No answer.

He called again: "Hello, Rock!"

Still no answer.

Three times the monkey called, and then he said: "Why is it, friend Rock, that you do not answer me tonight?"

"Oh," said the crocodile to himself, "the rock must talk to the monkey at night. I'll have to answer for the rock this time."

So he answered: "Yes, Monkey! What is it?"

The monkey laughed and said: "Oh, it's you, Crocodile, is it?"

"Yes," said the crocodile. "I am waiting here for you. And I am going to eat you up!"

"You have certainly caught me this time," said the monkey, sounding afraid. "There is no other way for me to go home. Open your mouth wide so I can jump right into it."

Now the monkey knew very well that when crocodiles open their mouths wide, they shut their eyes.

So while the crocodile lay on the rock with his mouth open and his eyes shut, the monkey jumped.

But not into his mouth!

He landed on the top of the crocodile's head, and then sprang quickly to the river bank.

Up he ran into his tree.

When the crocodile saw the trick the monkey had played on him, he said: "Monkey, I thought I was cunning, but you are much more cunning than I. And you know no fear. I will leave you alone after this."

"Thank you, Crocodile," said the monkey. "But I shall be on the watch for you just the same."

And so he was, and the crocodile never, never caught him.

Reader's Response ∼ If you could be either the monkey or the crocodile, which would you choose? Why?

Monkey Business

Monkeys are very clever animals. This monkey's name is Jo and she's special— she has a real job! Jo works as a live-in helper for a man who is paralyzed below his shoulders. She makes his life easier by

getting him what he needs, such as food, tapes, books, and the remote control for the TV. She was trained for her job by Dr. Mary Joan Willard and her team at Helping Hands, Simian Aides for the Disabled in Boston, Massachusetts.

Why did Jo get the job? She is a capuchin monkey. These monkeys are especially smart. They are also neat and eager to learn new skills. They can learn some tasks in as little as a half hour, but other jobs take hours to learn. A typical full-grown capuchin monkey weighs five pounds, is seventeen inches long, and lives to be about forty years old. Similar to dogs, they come to care about their owners and offer them friendship as well as help.

What other jobs might these clever monkeys learn to do that would help people with disabilities?

141

How Doth the

Little Crocodile

How doth the little crocodile
    Improve his shining tail,
And pour the waters of the Nile
    On every golden scale!

How cheerfully he seems to grin,
    How neatly spreads his claws,
And welcomes little fishes in,
    With gently smiling jaws!

Lewis Carroll

The House on East 88th Street

written and illustrated by Bernard Waber

This is the house. The house on East 88th
Street. It is empty now, but it won't be for long.
Strange sounds come from the house. Can you
hear them? Listen: SWISH, SWASH, SPLASH,
SWOOSH . . .

It began one sunny morning when the
Citywide Storage and Moving Company truck
pulled up to the house on East 88th Street and
unloaded the belongings of Mr. and Mrs.
Joseph F. Primm and their young son Joshua. It
was a trying day for everyone. Mrs. Primm just
couldn't decide where to put the piano. And Mr.
Primm's favorite pipe was accidentally packed
away in one of dozens of cartons lying about.

SWISH, SWASH, SPLASH, SWOOSH. Loudly and clearly the sounds now rumbled through the house. "It's only a little thunder," Mrs. Primm assured everyone. When a Citywide Storage and Moving man carried in their potted pistachio tree, everyone rejoiced; the truck was at last empty. The movers wished them well and hurried off to their next job for the day.

"Now, I'm going to prepare our lunch," announced Mrs. Primm. "But first I want to go upstairs and wash these grimy hands."

SWISH, SWASH, SPLASH, SWOOSH . . .

A puzzled Mrs. Primm stopped to listen. By and by her ears directed her to the bathroom door.

"What can it be?" she asked herself as she opened the door.

What she saw made her slam it quickly shut.

Mrs. Primm knew she was going to scream and just waited for it to happen. But she couldn't scream. She could scarcely even talk. The most Mrs. Primm was able to manage was the sharp hoarse whisper of a voice which she used to call Mr. Primm.

"Joseph," she said, "there's a crocodile in our bathtub."

Mr. Primm looked into the bathroom.

The next moment found them flying off in different directions.

"Help, help," Mrs. Primm cried out as she struggled with a window stuck with fresh paint.

"Operator, operator," Mr. Primm shouted into the telephone, and then he remembered that it was not yet connected.

147

Joshua, who had heard everything, raced to the front door, to be greeted there by an oddly dressed man who handed him a note. "This will explain everything about the crocodile," said the man, leaving quietly but swiftly.

Mr. Primm read the note:

Please be kind to my crocodile.
He is the most gentle of creatures
and would not do harm to a flea.
He must have tender, loving care,
for he is an artist and can perform
many good tricks. Perhaps he will
perform some for you.

I shall return.

Cordially,

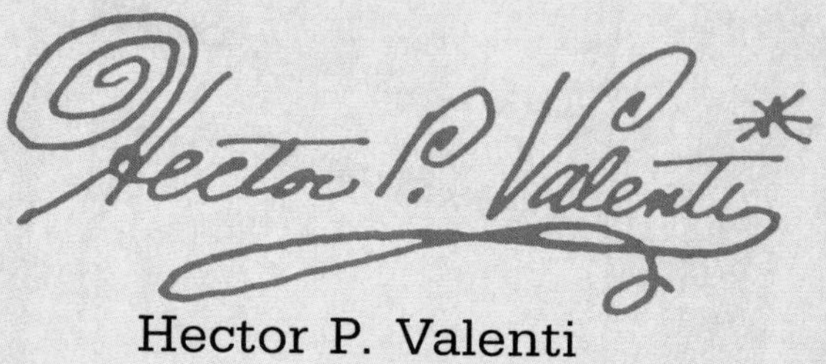

Hector P. Valenti

Hector P. Valenti
Star of stage and screen

P.S. He will eat only Turkish caviar.
P.P.S. His name is Lyle.

"Turkish caviar indeed," exclaimed Mrs. Primm. "Oh, to think this could happen on East 88th Street. Whatever will we do with him?"

Suddenly, before anyone could think of a worthy answer, there was Lyle.

And just as suddenly he got hold of a ball that had been lying among Joshua's belongings and began to balance it on his nose . . . and roll it down the notches of his spine.

Now he was walking on his front feet . . . and taking flying leaps.

Now he was twirling Joshua's hoop, doing it so expertly that the Primms just had to clap their hands and laugh.

Lyle bowed appreciatively.

He had won his way into their hearts and into their new home.

"Every home should have a crocodile," said Mrs. Primm one day.

"Lyle is one of the family now. He loves helping out with chores."

"He won't allow anyone else to carry out old newspapers . . . or take in the milk."

"He folds towels, feeds the bird, and when he sets the table there is always a surprise."

"I had only to show him once how to make up a bed."

"People everywhere stop to talk with him. They say he is the nicest crocodile they ever met."

"Lyle likes to play in the park. He always goes once around in the pony cart."

"And now he has learned to eat something besides Turkish caviar."

"Lyle is a good sport. Everyone wants him
to play on his side."

"He is wonderful company. We take him
everywhere."

"Just give him his Turkish caviar and his
bed of warm water and he is happy as a bird."

One day a brass band paraded past the
house on East 88th Street.

The Primm family rushed to the window to
watch. They called for Lyle, but there was no
answer.

"Look," someone pointed out. "It's Lyle,
he's in the parade."

There was Lyle doing his specialty of somersault, flying leaps, walking on front feet and taking bows just as he did the first day they laid eyes on him. The people watching cheered him on, while Lyle smiled back at them and blew kisses. A photographer was on hand to take pictures.

The next day Lyle was famous.

The telephone rang continually and bundles of mail were dropped by the door. One letter was from someone Lyle knew particularly well. Mr. Primm read it:

Just a few words to say
I shall return.

Cordially,

Hector P. Valenti
Star of stage and screen

P.S. Very soon.
P.P.S. To fetch my crocodile.

Several days later, Mrs. Primm and Lyle were in the kitchen shelling peas when they heard a knocking at the door.

It was Hector P. Valenti, star of stage and screen.

"I have come for Lyle," announced Signor Valenti.

"You can't have Lyle," cried Mrs. Primm, "he is very happy living here, and we love him dearly."

"Lyle must be returned to me," insisted Signor Valenti. "Was it not I who raised him from young crocodilehood? Was it not I who taught him his bag of tricks? We have appeared together on stages the world over."

"But why then did you leave him alone in a strange house?" asked Mrs. Primm.

"Because," answered Signor Valenti, "I could no longer afford to pay for his Turkish caviar. But now Lyle is famous and we shall be very rich." Mrs. Primm was saddened, but she knew Lyle properly belonged to Signor Valenti and she had to let him go.

It was a tearful parting for everyone.

Signor Valenti had big plans for Lyle. They were to travel far and wide . . . stay in many hotels . . . where sometimes the tubs were too big . . . and other times too small . . . or too crowded.

Signor Valenti did what he could to coax a smile from Lyle.

He tried making funny faces at him . . . he stood on his head. He tickled his toes and told him uproarious stories that in happier days would have had Lyle doubled over with laughter.

But Lyle could not laugh. Nor could he make people laugh. He made them cry instead . . . One night in Paris, he made an entire audience cry.

The theater manager was furious and ordered them off his stage.

Meanwhile at the house on East 88th Street, Mrs. Primm went about her work without her usual bright smile. And deep sighs could be heard coming from behind the newspaper Mr. Primm was reading.

Every morning Joshua anxiously awaited the arrival of the mailman in hope of receiving word from Lyle. One morning a letter did come. He knew the handwriting very well.

Just a few words to say
we shall return.

Cordially,

Hector P. Valenti

Hector P. Valenti
Former star of stage and screen

P.S. I am sick of crocodiles.
P.P.S. And the tears of crocodiles.

Not too many days after, the Primms were delighted to find Hector P. Valenti and Lyle at their door.

"Here, take him back," said Signor Valenti. "He is no good. He will never make anyone laugh again."

But Signor Valenti was very much mistaken.

Everyone laughed . . . and laughed . . . and laughed.

And in the end so did Signor Valenti.

So now if you should happen to be walking past the house on East 88th Street and if you should happen to hear sounds that go: SWISH, SWASH, SPLASH, SWOOSH! don't be surprised. It's only Lyle. Lyle the crocodile.

Reader's Response ~ How did you feel when Lyle left the Primms?

Library Link ~ *If you liked this story by Bernard Waber, you might enjoy reading some of his other books, such as* I Was All Thumbs, The Snake: A Very Long Story, *and* An Anteater Named Arthur.

GLOSSARY

Full pronunciation key* The pronunciation of each word is shown just after the word, in this way: **abbreviate** (ə brē′vē āt).

The letters and signs used are pronounced as in the words below.

The mark ′ is placed after a syllable with a primary or heavy accent as in the example above.

The mark ′ after a syllable shows a secondary or lighter accent, as in **abbreviation** (ə brē′vē ā′shən).

SYMBOL	KEY WORDS	SYMBOL	KEY WORDS	SYMBOL	KEY WORDS
a	ask, fat	u	up, cut	r	red, dear
ā	ape, date	ur	fur, fern	s	sell, pass
ä	car, father			t	top, hat
		ə	a in ago	v	vat, have
e	elf, ten		e in agent	w	will, always
er	berry, care		e in father	y	yet, yard
ē	even, meet		i in unity	z	zebra, haze
			o in collect		
i	is, hit		u in focus	ch	chin, arch
ir	mirror, here			n̂g	ring, singer
ī	ice, fire	b	bed, dub	sh	she, dash
		d	did, had	th	thin, truth
o	lot, pond	f	fall, off	*th*	then, father
ō	open, go	g	get, dog	zh	s in pleasure
ô	law, horn	h	he, ahead		
oi	oil, point	j	joy, jump	′	as in (ā′b′l)
oo	look, pull	k	kill, bake		
o͞o	ooze, tool	l	let, ball		
yoo	unite, cure	m	met, trim		
yo͞o	cute, few	n	not, ton		
ou	out, crowd	p	put, tap		

*Pronunciation key and respellings adapted from *Webster's New World Dictionary, Basic School Edition,* Copyright © 1983 by Simon & Schuster, Inc. Reprinted by permission.

A

a·board (ə bôrd′) *adverb*. on, in, or into a boat, train, airplane, or bus.

ad·ven·ture (əd ven′chər) *noun*. **1.** a dangerous event. **2.** an unusual or exciting experience. **adventures.**

am·ble (am′b'l) *verb*. **1.** to walk in a slow, easy way. **2.** to move slowly and smoothly by raising both legs on one side, then both legs on the other side: used to describe the way a horse, donkey, etc., moves. **ambled.**

an·chor (aṅg′kər) *noun*. a heavy object that is lowered into the water on a rope or chain to keep a boat from drifting, usually a metal piece with hooks that dig into the ground under the water.

ax·le (ak′s'l) *noun*. a bar or rod on which the wheels at each end turn: When the *axle* broke on the wagon, one wheel rolled down the hill.

B

be·lief (bə lēf′) *noun*. **1.** a thought or feeling that something is true or real; faith. **2.** anything accepted as true. **beliefs.**

bu·gle (byo͞o′g'l) *noun*. a type of small trumpet, usually without playing keys or valves.

bunk (buṅgk) *noun*. **1.** a built-in bed that hangs on a wall like a shelf. **2.** a narrow bed: The cowboy went to his *bunk* after a hard day's work.

C

ca·ble (kā′b'l) *noun*. **1.** a strong rope, usually made of covered wires or metal twisted together. **2.** a bundle of insulated wires that conduct electricity. **3.** a shorter word for *cablegram*, a telegraph message sent overseas.

aboard

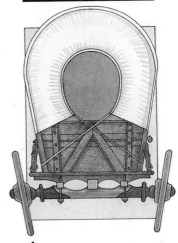

axle

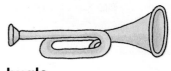

bugle

159

chicken

crocodile

deck

cav·i·ty (kav′ə tē) *noun.* **1.** a hollow open space, such as the hole caused by decay in a tooth: The children used the small *cavity* in the tree as a secret hiding place. **2.** a natural hollow, enclosed space in the body.

chat·ter (chat′ər) *verb.* **1.** to make short, quick noises that sound like talking: The birds were *chattering* outside the window. **2.** to talk fast and foolishly without stopping. **chattering.**

chick·en (chik′ən) *noun.* **1.** a young hen or rooster. **2.** the meat of a chicken. **chickens.**

choke (chōk) *verb.* **1.** to try to breathe when something is stuck in the windpipe. **2.** to squeeze the throat to stop breathing. **3.** to have trouble breathing. **choked.**

clam·ber (klam′bər) *verb.* to climb by trying hard, especially using both the hands and feet: The boy *clambered* up the tree. **clambered.**

con·ser·va·tion·ist (kon′sər vā′shən ist) *noun.* one who helps to preserve natural resources: The *conservationists* worked to save the forest when others wanted to cut it down. **conservationists.**

cour·age (kur′ij) *noun.* the ability to control fear in order to go through danger, pain, or trouble; bravery.

croc·o·dile (krok′ə dīl) *noun.* a large tropical lizard with thick skin, a long tail, a long, narrow, triangular head with large jaws, and cone-shaped teeth.

cun·ning (kun′iñg) *adjective.* clever; able to cheat or trick others: The *cunning* fox was able to fool the rabbit.

D

deck (dek) *noun.* **1.** the floor of a ship. **2.** a pack of 52 playing cards.

de·serve (di zurv′) *verb.* to have the right to something: We worked hard and we *deserve* the prize. **deserved.**

de·ter·mined (di tur′mənd) *adjective.* **1.** having your mind made up. **2.** strong and sure.

dif·fi·cult (dif′i kəlt) *adjective.* **1.** hard to do or make; causing a lot of trouble, thought, time, or practice; hard to understand. **2.** hard to get along with.

dis·o·bey (dis ə bā′) *verb.* to refuse to follow orders.

dis·tance (dis′təns) *noun*.
1. the amount of space between two points. **2.** a place far away.

dive (dīv) *verb*. **1.** to plunge headfirst into water. **2.** to go underwater to look for something. **3.** to move or drop suddenly. **dived.**

drawn (drôn) *verb*. to be pulled: The wagon was *drawn* by two horses.

E

ea·ger (ē′gər) *adjective*. wanting very much to do or get something.

ech·o (ek′ō) *noun*. a sound heard again after it bounces off a surface. —*verb*. to repeat. **echoed.**

ed·u·ca·tion (ej′ə kā′shən) *noun*. what you learn by being taught in school or by training.

en·dan·ger (in dān′jər) *verb*. **1.** to place in danger. **2.** to put in danger of becoming extinct, or dying out: An *endangered* animal is an animal that is scarce, or hard to find, anywhere in the world. **endangered.**

endangered species a species of animal or plant that is scarce, or in danger of becoming extinct: We have

to protect an *endangered species,* such as the American bald eagle, or it will disappear from the earth forever.

en·gi·neer (en′jə nir′) *noun*. a person who is trained to plan and build machines, roads, bridges, etc. **engineers.**

Eng·lish (iñg′glish) *adjective*. of England, its language, or its people.

F

fa·mil·iar (fə mil′yər) *adjective*. **1.** close; friendly; knowing someone or something well. **2.** acting too friendly in a pushy way. **3.** ordinary or usual.

fi·ber·glass (fī′bər glas′) *noun*. material made of glass threads that is used to make cloth, insulation, boats, etc.

fish·er·man (fish′ər mən) *noun*. someone who catches or tries to catch fish for sport or for a living. **fishermen.**

freight train (frāt trān) *noun*. a train that carries a load of goods. **freight trains.**

fu·ture (fyoo′chər) *noun*. a time that is to come: In the *future*, I will study more for tests.

a fat	oi oil	ch chin
ā ape	oo look	sh she
ä car, father	oo tool	th thin
e ten	ou out	th then
er care	u up	zh leisure
ē even	ur fur	ñg ring
i hit		
ir here	ə = a *in* ago	
ī bite, fire	e *in* agent	
o lot	i *in* unity	
ō go	o *in* collect	
ô law, horn	u *in* focus	

engineer

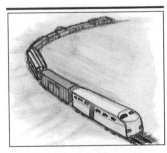

freight train

hoot owl

Hoot is a good example of a word that is taken directly from a sound. The word *hoot* in *hoot owl* sounds like the call of an owl.

iceberg

G

gal·ley (gal'ē) *noun*. **1.** a long, low ship used long ago, moved by sails and oars. **2.** the kitchen of a boat or ship: The sailor went to the *galley* to start cooking.

glit·ter (glit'ər) *verb*. to shine with a sparkling light. **glittered.**

H

hatch (hach) *verb*. **1.** to bring forth baby animals, such as birds, fish, turtles, etc. from eggs. **2.** to break out of the egg. **— hatchling** *noun*. a newborn animal that has just come out of its egg: The *hatchlings* opened their eyes and looked at their mother for the first time. **hatchlings.**

hoot owl (hoōt oul) *noun*. a bird with a large head, large eyes, small hooked beak, and sharp claws. It makes a long, low sound.

hur·ri·cane (hur'ə kān) *noun*. a storm with strong winds blowing in a circle at 73 miles per hour or more, usually with heavy rains.

I

ice·berg (īs'bʉrg) *noun*. a huge piece of ice, floating in the sea: Most of an *iceberg* is under the water.

i·cy (ī'sē) *adjective*. **1.** covered with ice; frozen or slippery. **2.** feeling very cold like ice.

in·stinc·tive (in stiñgk'tiv) *adjective*. caused or done by a natural way of acting or feeling that exists from birth. **—instinctively** *adverb:* The newborn sea turtles *instinctively* went to the safety of the ocean.

J

jun·gle (juñg'g'l) *noun*. land in warm, moist parts of the world, covered with trees, plants, and vines.

K

kind·ness (kīnd'nis) *noun*. the habit or way of being friendly, good, generous, etc., to others.

L

lad·en (lād″n) *adjective*. having or carrying a heavy load: After a busy day of shopping, Mother left the department store *laden* with packages.

lull (lul) *verb*. **1.** to make or become calm or quiet. **2.** to calm by using soft sounds or movements. **lulled.**

lum·i·nous (lo͞o′mə nəs) *adjective*. **1.** giving off light; shining. **2.** full of light, shiny: When ocean waves reflect the moonlight, they appear *luminous,* or shiny. **3.** glowing in the dark. **4.** clear; easily understood.

M

man·age (man′ij) *verb*. **1.** to be in charge of. **2.** to be sure that things get done in workplaces, homes, etc. **3.** to succeed in doing something: She *managed* to swim across the lake. **managed.**

man·do·lin (man′d′l in) *noun*. a musical instrument with eight or ten strings played with a pick.

man·go (maṇ̂g′gō) *noun*. **1.** a tropical fruit with a yellowish-red thick skin and a hard pit inside. **2.** the tree on which this fruit grows.

med·al (med″l) *noun*. a piece of metal with words or pictures on it, usually given as a prize to people who do something special.

mes·quite (mes kēt′ or mes′kēt) *noun*. a kind of tree or shrub with thorns and sugary, beanlike pods that are often used to feed animals.

mil·lion (mil′yən) *noun*. one thousand thousands (1,000,000). **millions.**

min·is·ter (min′is tər) *noun*. the head of a church, especially a Protestant church; a religious leader. **ministers.**

mis·chief (mis′chif) *noun*. **1.** harm, damage, or injury. **2.** an act that causes harm. **3.** a person, especially a child, who bothers people or things. **4.** playful tricks: He is always getting into *mischief* when his mother is busy.

a fat	oi oil	ch chin
ā ape	o͞o look	sh she
ä car, father	o͞o tool	th thin
e ten	ou out	th then
er care	u up	zh leisure
ē even	ur fur	ṇ̂g ring
i hit		
ir here	ə = a *in* ago	
ī bite, fire	e *in* agent	
o lot	i *in* unity	
ō go	o *in* collect	
ô law, horn	u *in* focus	

laden

medal

mule

mustang

nuzzle

mix·ture (miks′chər) *noun.* something made by blending different things into a single, whole thing.

mor·sel (môr′s'l) *noun.* a small bit of food.

most·ly (mōst′lē) *adverb.* for the greater part; mainly.

mule (myo͞ol) *noun.* **1.** an animal whose parents are a horse and a donkey. **2.** a person who is stubborn. *used only in informal language.*

mus·tang (mus′tañg) *noun.* a small, wild horse that usually runs free in some parts of the western United States. **mustangs.**

N

ne·glect (ni glekt′) *verb.* **1.** not to take care of as one should: He *neglected* to walk the dog yesterday. **2.** to take little notice of. **neglected.**

neigh·bor·hood (nā′bər ho͝od) *noun.* **1.** a small part of a city, town, etc.: My school is in my *neighborhood*. **2.** people who live near each other.

nuz·zle (nuz″l) *verb.* **1.** to rub with the nose: The dog *nuzzled* the puppy. **2.** to lie close and be comfortable. **nuzzled.**

O

o·cean·og·ra·pher (ō′shə nog′rə fər) *noun.* a person who studies the oceans and the animals and plants that live in them: The *oceanographers* rushed to help the pilot whales that had beached themselves in the shallow bay. **oceanographers.**

P

palm frond (päm frond) *noun.* the large leaf at the top of a palm tree: We cut *palm fronds* to make a roof for our hut. **palm fronds.**

per·suade (pər swād′) *verb.* to get someone to act or think in a certain way by making it seem like a good thing.

pil·grim (pil′grəm) *noun.*
1. a person who travels to places away from home for religious reasons. **2. Pilgrim.** one of the group of Puritans who left England and settled in Plymouth, Massachusetts, in 1620. **Pilgrims.**

pi·lot (pī′lət) *noun.* **1.** a person who steers a ship.
2. a person who flies an airplane or helicopter.

plan·et (plan′it) *noun.* a large heavenly body that moves in an orbit or path around a star.

plunge (plunj) *verb.* **1.** to throw or push with great power. **2.** to dive. **plunged.**

pop·u·lar (pop′yə lər) *adjective.* **1.** having many friends; very well liked.
2. liked by a lot of people.

pred·a·tor (pred′ə tôr) *noun.*
1. an animal that lives by killing and eating other animals: Many animals have to hide their eggs to keep them from being eaten by *predators.* **2.** one that lives by robbing, stealing, etc. **predators.**

pre·pare (pri par′) *verb.* **1.** to make or get ready: He can't go with us because he has to *prepare* for a test. **2.** to put something together.

pro·vide (prə vīd′) *verb.* **1.** to give what is needed. **2.** to support. **3.** to get ready ahead of time. **provided.**

purr (pur) *verb.* to make the soft sound a cat makes when it is happy. **purred.**

a fat	oi oil	ch chin
ā ape	oo look	sh she
ä car, father	o͞o tool	th thin
e ten	ou out	*th* then
er care	u up	zh leisure
ē even	ur fur	ng ring
i hit		
ir here	ə = a *in* ago	
ī bite, fire	e *in* agent	
o lot	i *in* unity	
ō go	o *in* collect	
ô law, horn	u *in* focus	

R

rack·et (rak′it) *verb.* to make a loud, clattering noise. **racketing.**

ra·di·o (rā′dē o′) *noun.* **1.** a way that sounds are sent from one place to another by changing them into electrical waves that travel through the air. **2.** a receiving set that picks up those waves and changes them back into sound.

re·li·gion (ri lij′ən) *noun.* **1.** a belief in God or gods. **2.** a way of living by worshiping God.

re·li·gious (re lij′əs) *adjective.*
1. showing belief in God or a religion. **2.** having to do with religion.

re·ply (ri plī′) *verb.* to answer in words or in actions: Susan *replied* to his letter right away. **replied.**

planet

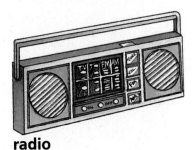

radio

shipwreck

re·ward (ri wôrd′) *noun*.
1. something given in return for good work. **2.** money given for finding and returning something that was lost.

S

Sonar is an acronym. An acronym is a word that is made by putting together the first letters of a longer name or description. Sonar comes from *so*und *na*vigation *r*anging.

submarine

schol·ar (skol′ər) *noun*. **1.** a person who learns a lot by studying. **2.** a person who goes to school or studies with a teacher. **3.** a student who enjoys study and learning.

sci·en·tist (sī′ən tist) *noun*. a person who is an expert in a particular branch of science, such as biology, agriculture, etc. **scientists.**

scold (skōld) *verb*. to tell someone what he or she is doing wrong in an angry voice: He *scolded* me for arriving late for class. **scolded.**

shim·mer (shim′ər) *verb*. to shine with a wavering kind of light: The puddle of water on the sidewalk was *shimmering* under the street light. **shimmering.**

ship·wreck (ship′rek) *noun*. the parts of a ship left after it is destroyed or lost at sea.

shiv·er (shiv′ər) *verb*. to shake as when you are very cold or afraid; to tremble. **shivered.**

so·nar (sō′när) *noun*. a machine that sends sound waves through water to locate objects; used to find submarines, measure the depth of the ocean, etc.

spar·kle (spär′k′l) *verb*. to shine as if giving off sparks or flashes of light. **sparkled.**

spe·cies (spē′shēz) *noun*. **1.** a group of related plants or animals that are alike in certain ways; a group of living things that produce living things of the same kind: All dogs are the same *species* because they all produce baby dogs, or puppies. **2.** a kind or sort.

sput·ter (sput′ər) *verb*. **1.** to spit out food or water from your mouth when speaking. **2.** to talk in a fast, excited way. **3.** to make hissing or popping noises. **sputtered.**

stal·lion (stal′yən) *noun*. a full-grown male horse that can have offspring: The wild *stallion* galloped across the plains.

sub·ma·rine (sub′mə rēn) *noun*. a kind of ship that travels underwater and can stay there for a long time.

sur·vive (sər vīv′) *verb*. to stay alive under bad conditions.

T

tel·e·vi·sion (tel′ə vizh′ən) *noun*. **1.** a way of sending pictures by changing them into electrical waves that travel through the air. **2.** a receiving set for images and sounds.

thrash (thrash) *verb*. **1.** to hit with a stick, whip, or other object. **2.** to move around wildly or without control: The fish *thrashed* around in the shallow water. **thrashed.**

thump (thump) *noun*. **1.** a blow or hit made by something heavy. **2.** the sound made by such a blow.

tour·isty (toor′ist ē) *adjective*. about people who travel for pleasure. *used only in informal language.*

tre·men·dous (tri men′dəs) *adjective*. **1.** very large or huge. **2.** surprisingly wonderful, amazing, etc.

W

wasp (wosp *or* wôsp) *noun*. a flying insect, with a slender body and a narrow waist, that stings. **wasps.**

wa·ter·fall (wôt′ər fôl) *noun*. a natural stream of water that falls from a high place such as a cliff.

weap·on (wep′ən) *noun*. something used for fighting such as a club, gun, etc. **weapons.**

week·ly (wēk′lē) *adjective*. happening or appearing once a week or every week.

wheel·ing (hwēl′iṅg) *verb*. turning around in a circular motion.

whin·ny (hwin′ē) *verb*. to make the low neighing sound that a horse makes. **whinnied.**

wor·ship (wur′ship) *noun*. **1.** a church service; prayer. **2.** great love or admiration of any kind. —*verb*. **1.** to offer prayers; attend church. **2.** to show great love or admiration.

worst (wurst) *adjective*. the most bad, harmful, etc.; least good.

Y

yowl (youl) *verb*. to howl or cry out in a long, sad way.

a fat	oi oil	ch chin
ā ape	o͝o look	sh she
ä car, father	o͞o tool	th thin
e ten	ou out	*th* then
er care	u up	zh leisure
ē even	ur fur	ṅg ring
i hit		
ir here	ə = a *in* ago	
ī bite, fire	e *in* agent	
o lot	i *in* unity	
ō go	o *in* collect	
ô law, horn	u *in* focus	

Television is a new word, when compared to most of the words we use. It came into use seventy years ago, when television was first being developed. The word means "seeing at a distance."

wasp

ABOUT THE
Authors & *Illustrators*

GEORGE ANCONA

▲ George Ancona grew up in Coney Island, studied in Mexico, and now lives in Stony Point, New York. He feels that curiosity is the biggest element in his work. Mr. Ancona says, "Photographing, filming or writing about someone or someplace is my way of feeling alive and in touch with the world around me." His photographs have appeared in over three dozen children's books and have been exhibited at Lincoln Center and the Museum of Modern Art in New York City. *(Born 1929)*

EDWARD ARDIZZONE

✳ Edward Ardizzone was born in Indochina, which is called Vietnam today. When he was five years old, he moved to England with his mother and sisters, where he lived the rest of his life. He said it was his children's pleas of "Daddy, please, please tell us a story" and "Daddy, please, draw us a picture of two elephants having a fight" that led him to create his books and illustrations. Edward Ardizzone won many awards for his books, including the *New York Times* Best Illustrated Book Award in 1962, 1973, and 1980. *(1900–1979)*

LEWIS CARROLL

■ Lewis Carroll's real name was Charles Lutwidge Dodgson. He taught mathematics in England, but he is best known for his book *Alice's Adventures in Wonderland*. He made up the stories about Alice to tell to the children of a friend. The girls liked the stories so much, they asked him to write them down. Later, he wrote another book about Alice. It is called *Through the Looking Glass*. (1832–1898)

LYDIA MARIA CHILD

▲ Lydia Maria Child was born in Medford, Massachusetts. She was the youngest of six children. Her father was a baker. He made "Medford Crackers," which were very popular. He was able to give all his children a good education. Lydia Maria Child started the first U.S. magazine for children. She also wrote novels, books of games for children, and many articles against slavery. (1802–1880)

VALERIE FLOURNOY

❋ Valerie Flournoy was graduated from William Smith College and now lives in New York City. In addition to *The Patchwork Quilt*, she has written two other books for children, *The Best Time of Day* and *The Twins Strike Back*. When she is not working, Ms. Flournoy likes to visit classrooms to talk with children about writing, reading, and staying in school.

PAUL GALDONE

✳ Paul Galdone was born in Budapest, Hungary. He and his family moved to the United States in 1928. He had a difficult time in school because he did not speak English well. He liked biology class, however, because he could draw grasshoppers. "I was soon drawing them for all the other pupils," he said. Mr. Galdone has twice been the runner-up for the Caldecott Medal. *(1914–1986)*

JAN SPIVEY GILCHRIST

▲ Jan Spivey Gilchrist was born in Chicago, Illinois. She has taught in the public schools in Illinois and Massachusetts but now works only as an illustrator. When Lessie Jones Little's publisher needed an illustrator for her book *Children of Long Ago*, her daughter, author Eloise Greenfield, recommended Ms. Gilchrist for the job. Jan Spivey Gilchrist called it "the most wonderful opportunity of my life."

HELEN V. GRIFFITH

■ Helen V. Griffith says, "I have been writing and drawing since I could handle a pencil.... When I was very young I wrote poetry, usually about animals." She has always liked animals, and a dog has had a featured role in many of her books. "I don't begin by thinking, 'I'm going to write about a dog,' but that's what happens." *(Born 1934)*

RACHEL ISADORA

✳ Rachel Isadora was a ballet dancer before she became an artist. She began dancing professionally when she was eleven years old but had to retire several years later because she injured her foot. She then turned to drawing as a career. Today, Rachel Isadora is an award-winning author and illustrator. Her book *Ben's Trumpet* is a Caldecott Honor Book and a Boston Globe Horn Book Honor book.

LESSIE JONES LITTLE

▲ Lessie Jones Little started writing when she was sixty-seven years old. She was a great-grandmother. She has published two books for children with her daughter, Eloise Greenfield. *I Can Do It Myself* is a book about gaining self-confidence. *Childtimes: A Three Generation Memoir,* a story about her family, was a Boston Globe Horn Book Honor book for nonfiction in 1980. Ms. Little died in 1986.

LILIAN MOORE

■ Lilian Moore was born in New York City. As a schoolteacher, she taught children who had been out of school and did not know how to read. Because she could not find interesting books for these children to read, she wrote her own books for them. She has written more than forty books since then.

JERRY PINKNEY

✳ Jerry Pinkney uses both photographs and live models for his drawings. He says he bought an old hand-stitched quilt from the 1890s to use as a model for the illustrations in *The Patchwork Quilt*. Mr. Pinkney also designs postage stamps, such as the Harriet Tubman, Martin Luther King, Jr., and Benjamin Banneker stamps in the "Black Heritage" series. *(Born 1939)*

ELIZABETH SHUB

▲ Elizabeth Shub was born in Poland. She came to the United States when she was a child. She writes books for children and also translates books into English for other writers. She helped Isaac Bashevis Singer translate *Zlateh the Goat and Other Stories* from Yiddish. One of the books she has written for children is *Seeing is Believing*.

JAMES STEVENSON

■ James Stevenson is a writer and illustrator. Although he began his career as a cartoonist and artist, he always wanted to be a writer. He has written many books for young people. Several of his books have been chosen as American Library Association Notable Books. *(Born 1929)*

YOSHIKO UCHIDA

❋ Yoshiko Uchida wrote books about Japan and its people and about Japanese Americans as well. She said, "I wanted American children to become familiar with the marvelous Japanese folk tales I had heard in my childhood. I wanted them to read about Japanese children, learning to understand and respect differences in customs and culture, but realizing also that basically human beings are alike the world over, with similar joys and hopes." *(1921–1992)*

BERNARD WABER

▲ Since Bernard Waber started writing and illustrating the Lyle books, his house has become almost like a museum of crocodile things. He says there are stuffed toy crocodiles on "tables, sofas, stairs, floors, or whatever surface is diminishingly available. A claw-footed bathtub ... identical to the one shared at the Primm household ... sits in our foyer together with its obligatory stuffed, Lyle-type occupant." *(Born 1924)*

AUTHOR INDEX